MW01012882

Warrior • 123

Soviet Rifleman
1941–45

Gordon L Rottmann • Illustrated by Howard Gerrard

First published in Great Britain in 2007 by Osprey Publishing,
Midland House, West Way, Botley, Oxford OX2 0PH, UK
443 Park Avenue South, New York, NY 10016, USA
E-mail: info@ospreypublishing.com

A CIP catalog record for this book is available from the British Library

ISBN: 978 1 84603 127 4

Page layout by Scribe, Oxford.
Index by Alison Worthington
Typeset in Helvetica Neue and ITC New Baskerville
Originated by PDQ Digital Media Solutions
Printed in China through Worldprint

07 08 09 10 11   10 9 8 7 6 5 4 3 2 1

FOR A CATALOG OF ALL BOOKS PUBLISHED BY OSPREY MILITARY AND
AVIATION PLEASE CONTACT:

NORTH AMERICA
Osprey Direct, c/o Random House Distribution Center, 400 Hahn Road,
Westminster, MD 21157
E-mail: info@ospreydirect.com

ALL OTHER REGIONS
Osprey Direct UK, P.O. Box 140 Wellingborough, Northants, NN8 2FA, UK
E-mail: info@ospreydirect.co.uk

www.ospreypublishing.com

Artist's note

Readers may care to note that the original paintings from
which the color plates in this book were prepared are
available for private sale. All reproduction copyright
whatsoever is retained by the Publishers. All inquiries
should be addressed to:

Howard Gerrard
11 Oaks Road
Tenterden
Kent
TN30 6RD
UK

The Publishers regret that they can enter into no
correspondence upon this matter.

Editor's note

Images not credited in this book are in the public domain.

Glossary

banya	steam bath
frontovik	front fighter, an informal term for the Soviet rifleman fighting at the frontline
kolkhoz	short for *kollektivnoe khoziaistvo* (collective farms)
makhorka	a poor, cheap, finely chopped tobacco
Narkom 100-gramm	People's Commissariat of Defense 100-gram; the supposed daily issue of vodka
NKVD	Narodny Komissariat Vnutrennikh Del (The People's Commissariat of Internal Affairs)
politruk	a deputy commander for political affairs
shapka-ushanka	fur cap
shchi	a cabbage soup made with meat broth
telogreika	padded jacket for winter wear Professional standing army troops

CONTENTS

SOVIET RIFLEMAN 1941-45

INTRODUCTION

When the German armies poured across eastern Poland and into the Union of Soviet Socialist Republics (USSR) on June 22, 1941, it found a massive army of 9 million troops organized within 303 divisions. Although well armed with artillery and tanks, this formidable army soon melted away under the Teutonic onslaught. A number of units fought bravely, but most folded and retreated deep within the Soviet Union. In the first two months of the war some 20,000 armored vehicles were lost, a total six times greater than the number of tanks possessed by the Germans. The air forces were largely destroyed on the ground, and some 4 million men were lost in combat or as prisoners of war (POWs) – 80 percent of the total strength of the USSR's armed forces. Yet the Soviet military held, and gradually turned the tide against the invaders to drive them back to Berloga – the "beast's lair" – Berlin.

The Raboche-Krest'yanskaya-Krasnaya Armiya (Red Army of Workers and Peasants; RKKA), while massive and well equipped, was a lumbering great bear of an army in the summer of 1941. It had performed well in a small-scale Siberian border clash with Japan in 1939, but its invasion of eastern Poland in the same year had been less than extraordinary. The western Ukraine and the Balkan States were seized in 1939–40, and although it eventfully won the 1939–40 Winter War with Finland, its humiliating initial defeats against a poorly equipped and much smaller army reinforced Hitler's perception that the cumbersome, overstuffed Red Army was ill prepared to face the Blitzkrieg offensive. To complicate matters further, from May 1937 to May 1938 Stalin had unleashed a far-reaching purge of officers at all levels of command. In many instances the most able commanders were executed en masse and the cowed remnants were often weak and incapable of dealing with the German forces about to slam into them.

As losses mounted, armies dissolved, and the Germans pushed deeper into Mother Russia, official attitudes began to change. The draconian methods used to keep units at the front lines, the relentless and often unfair punishment of those

Workers' Militia troops move through a wrecked factory. They went into battle bearing only one piece of military equipment, a rifle. In the early days regular Red Army units sometimes entered combat wearing working clothes. (Nik Cornish Collection L104)

who faltered, and the abuse inflicted on troops and civilians alike by the Communist Party apparatus were endured and the Red Army rebounded. With the aid of wide-ranging propaganda and the realization that the Germans would stop at nothing short of destroying the Motherland, the workers and peasants began to fight back, with a vengeance.

Factories poured out weapons, munitions, supplies, and equipment. New formations were built and the shattered remnants of defeated forces absorbed. Eventually American Lend-Lease materiel and British equipment was flowing into the beleaguered nation. Sacrifice, suffering, and loss were the rule rather than the exception in what became known as the Great Patriotic War.

Though embracing the principles of combined-arms mobile warfare backed by massed artillery, the Red Army was still largely an infantry force. The Red Army did not refer to its ground combat troops as "infantry," but as *streltsi* (rifle troops). The designation goes back to the Czarist era when rifle units were considered more elite than *pyekhoty* (rank-and-file infantry). The rifleman himself was known informally as a *peshkon* (lit. "on foot") or more commonly as a *frontovik* (front fighter). *Frontovik* was not a term equating to the American "GI," the British "Tommy," or the German *Landser* – these were general terms for soldiers, while the *frontovik* title was reserved for troops fighting in the front lines. In total 75 percent of all Russian divisions were designated as "rifle" and these *frontoviki* gradually began to turn the tide against the German onslaught. The sacrifices were tremendous and the losses staggering. The savage fighting to ensure the survival of the Motherland and the Communist Party lasted a total of three years, ten months, and 17 days. Some 20 million Russian citizens from over 100 different ethnic groups would die defending the largest nation on earth, but no one's sacrifice was more crucial to success than that of the frontline rifleman.

For the burned cities and villages,
For the deaths of our children and
  our mothers,
For the torture and humiliation
  of our people;
I swear revenge upon the enemy.
I swear that I would rather die
  in battle with the enemy than
  surrender my people and my
  country to the fascist invaders!
Blood for blood!
Death for death!

From a Soviet motivational poster

CONSCRIPTION

The conscription system

"[The] defense of the Motherland is the sacred duty of every citizen of the USSR." So declared the 1936 Constitution of the USSR. It further stated that "universal military service is law" and "military service in the Red Army of Workers and Peasants is an honorable duty."

Military service was a fact of life for the physically and mentally fit in the "workers' paradise" that was the USSR. Not only was it a constitutional duty for all citizens, but it was also clearly specified in the 1939 Law of Compulsory Military Service, which stated that all able-bodied males were eligible for conscription on reaching the age of 19. By 1939 the Soviet Union was already on a war footing. Only those enrolled in secondary or technical schools could have their service deferred. The same applied to the chronically ill. Such deferments were granted for 3–12 months, and could only be granted a maximum of three times. Those under arrest, deported to Siberia, or deprived of their suffrage rights were exempt from conscription, as were those with serious physical defects. Certain categories of specialists were also exempt: these included skilled workers (especially those in remote rural areas), scientists, rural school teachers, relocated farmers (forced to work on collective farms), and essential

Women were pressed into Workers' Militia units and saw frontline service. There were, however, no all-female infantry units in regular service. The woman to the left is armed with a 7.62mm PPD-40 submachine gun.

factory workers and technicians. The mentally deficient were exempted and militia (police) records were checked for possible enemies of the State unworthy of bearing arms. Only on reaching the age of 50 were Russian men exempt from military service.

Prior to the war there were three forms of military service: active duty, extended leave (commanders) and furlough (NCOs and lower ranks), and reserve duty. Leave and furlough were granted to commanders and soldiers who had completed active duty, or before completing five years' active duty if their services were not required. They were still on the rolls, but could return home and accept civilian employment, although they technically remained under military regulations and could be recalled immediately. Personnel placed on reserve duty had completed their active service or a combination of active duty and leave/furlough. Typically, a private would serve two years' active duty and three years on furlough, and then be assigned to the reserves until age 50. Sergeants served three years' active duty and two years' furlough. A soldier could extend his active service in five-year intervals, and could be retained on active duty two months beyond his release date. Of course, in times of war service was extended beyond any peacetime limits – deferments could be canceled, the age of reservists increased to 60, and all reservists were eligible for mobilization. Volunteers were also accepted and large numbers of idealistic young men signed up prior to and in the first couple of months of the war, especially from the cities where conditions were cramped and shortages prevailed. A new Conscription Act was passed on August 31, 1941, and the conscription age was lowered to 18 for those without secondary education and 19 for those educated to that level.

The average soldier had no inkling of the vast bureaucratic system that called him to military service. The system was purely statistical, based on the numbers and categories of troops needed by the field forces. Conscription was administered by over 20 military districts, each of which could in theory raise an army. The districts coincided with the *oblasts* (regions), the primary administrative subdivision of the USSR, although a district could encompass more than one *oblast* depending on the population density. *Oblasts* bore no relationship to the boundaries of the union republics and autonomous republics comprising the USSR and could be further subdivided into *raions* – countries.

It was from the *raion* military commissar that men received their draft notifications. Each *raion* was given quotas and the numbers of specialists necessary. The better-qualified men were often assigned to the Narodny Komissariat Vnutrennikh Del (The People's Commissariat of Internal Affairs; NKVD), the vast internal security organization, while the Red Army often had to make do with substandard recruits. Studies showed that many conscripts, especially from rural areas, had a vocabulary of just 500–2,000 words.

With the German invasion the system soon fell apart, especially in the more populous west, as Soviet territory was occupied and the government fell into turmoil. Huge numbers of potential soldiers were lost to the occupation. Those that fled east were eventually conscripted within the Red Army. They were under no administrative system, however, as their home records were lost. The NKVD rounded up undocumented men and turned them over to the Red Army. The difficult situation and lack of time prevented any more organized system from developing. The situation was so desperate that soon after the invasion ten divisions were raised in Siberian Gulags using 130,000 convicts.

Women were employed as *Rukovodstvo* (traffic controllers), an important job. This soldier wears the effective gray felt winter boots. (Nik Cornish Collection L27)

As the war progressed, former German-occupied areas were liberated and the inhabitants became liable for conscription. However, there was widespread distrust of these *Zapadniki* (Westerners) owing to their having been under German control. Many of the territories, the western Ukraine and the Baltic states for example, had only been absorbed into the USSR just prior to the war and the inhabitants, while glad to be relieved of German occupation, were by no means enthralled to see the return of Soviet domination. The NKVD screened potential army recruits and agents made inquiries as to their demonstrated loyalties to the Motherland during the occupation. Even partisans were screened. Those deemed politically unreliable were "reeducated" or simply sent to the Gulags instead of reporting for active duty with the Red Army.

The typical Red Army recruit

In a country as vast as the USSR, with its melting pot of ethnicities, there was no typical Red Army conscript or recruit. A *Krasnoarmeets* (lit. "Red Army Man") could be from a large city, town, village, or a remote rural area. He might have been uneducated or, if he had just graduated from school, most likely had never held a job. If not conscripted out of school he might have worked in a factory or shop, as a laborer, in the service industry, or in any number of other jobs. Many were agricultural workers. Forestry, mining, petroleum, and transportation were other major industries.

Numerous conscripts were raised on *kollektivnoe khoziaistvo* (collective farms) – *kolkhoz* for short. The *kolkhoz* was a state-owned agricultural cooperative where peasants, typically in units of 75 families, under the direction of Party-approved plans and "elected" leadership, were paid wages based on the quantity and quality of their work contribution and the success of their harvest. Each family could "own" a small plot of land for gardening, which remained part of the *kolkhoz*, and a few head of livestock. Forced collectivization was implemented between 1929 and 1937, and while resisted in some areas, particularly the Ukraine, it was welcomed by many serfs. Previously much of the land was owned by *kulaks*, "wealthy" serfs who owned farms, sawmills, dairies, and so forth, or privately owned motorized machinery, and may have rented out land. Collectivization destroyed the *kulaks* and redistributed the land. The former *kolkhoznik* soldier was particularly reliant on the cradle-to-grave benefits given by the Soviet state.

Conscription-age soldiers had been born in the early and mid-1920s. They knew nothing of a pre-communist Russia. They had been raised on a steady diet of state propaganda, dictates, and ever-changing regulations. News, information, and history were controlled by the government – their view of the outside world was a result of what the state told them. They lived in a nation in danger of "capitalist encirclement," with enemies on all sides. The reality was that the "worker's paradise" was below the European average in education, health care, standard of living, agricultural and industrial production, everything except for quantity of military hardware. There were shortages of everything. The country was run by a bloated, centralized bureaucracy pouring scarce resources into a lumbering military machine, acting under fear of external enemies and of a secret police searching for enemies within.

Becoming a Red Army rifleman
Prior to the war, mass conscription was conducted over two or three months at the beginning of the year. Call-up notices mailed out by the district military commissariat directed conscripts and reservists to report to an assembly point, often a local school. Typically they walked to the assembly point with a cardboard suitcase or bag containing a set of spare clothes and underwear, toilet articles, tobacco, and maybe socks, as many had been told they would be issued less desirable footwraps. They were given a quick physical examination and transported by train to mobilization reception centers operated by the military districts. It was the first train ride for many of the recruits. Many reported in drunk from farewell celebrations and this was indeed encouraged, as they were easier to manage while sleeping it off on the train.

At the military district reception center the conscripts turned in their civilian clothes to be mailed home, underwent another physical, heads were shaved, and they were given a *banya* (steam bath) to rid them of lice. Uniforms, typically ill-fitting, were issued. The issue was one or two uniforms, two sets of long underwear, cap, belt, boots, greatcoat, and footwraps. Care and cleaning of his uniform was the soldier's responsibility, except for the underwear – this was exchanged every ten days, usually longer in practice, for a washed set that had been worn by someone else. It was often said that the only two things that fitted were the boots and footwraps. One of the first things the recruits learned from a sergeant or

A dismounted cavalry unit serving as infantry. Cossacks and some other cavalrymen traditionally wore dark blue breeches. (Nik Cornish Collection L106)

recalled reservist was how apply footwraps to minimize creases. Their first ten days were spent in quarantine from other troops.

Riflemen (Specialty Code 133) would be issued most of their individual equipment, but probably not a weapon – there were too few firearms and they had to be shared during training. Besides cartridge pouches, a water bottle, shelter-cape, ration bag, and cooking pot, the conscript might be issued a canvas field clothing bag. He might not be issued an entrenching tool and gas mask until assigned to a combat unit.

The recruit would possibly also be issued with an identity tube. This was a 0.75in. diameter, 2.5in. long eight-sided black Bakelite tube with a screw-on cap. Later in the war they were made of black-painted wood. The tube contained a long narrow form on which 19 entries served as a personal record with information such as name, date of birth, unit number (sequential serial numbers were not assigned), parents' names and address, date of conscription/enlistment, promotions, wounds, etc. The tube was carried in a pocket. Soldiers were also issued a Red Army Pass, a 3x4in. tan or red booklet containing basic personal data to be carried at all times.

TRAINING AND TACTICS

Pre-conscription training
In theory students received a degree of pre-military training while still at school. As early as 1st grade, instruction began with physical training and motivational indoctrination one hour a week, which increased to

ten hours by 10th grade. A two-week pre-military summer camp was attended in 8th and 9th grades. Training continued through 10th grade and upon graduation students received a "Maturity Certificate" stating their eligibility for military service. In secondary (8th–10th grade) and vocational schools, instruction was provided in basic military skills thought sufficient to prepare boys to function as members of a platoon. This instruction included physical fitness, drill, military sports, skiing, marksmanship, chemical defense, scouting, sentry and messenger duties, section (squad) attack and defense, actions against tanks, first aid, military orientation, and history. Girls were taught military skills, but they were not expected to become frontline soldiers and so the training was focused on other key roles, such as medics or telegraphers.

The average boy may or may not have been enthused about pre-military training. Instruction was provided by reserve officers and sergeants and its quality and completeness varied. Much of the instruction was by lecture only, with limited hands-on training owing to scarce equipment and training facilities. In rural areas it may have been non-existent. In cities and large towns it was more effective, especially if there was a military base nearby from which instructors and equipment might be borrowed.

Youths could also join the OSOAVIAHIM (Union of Societies of Assistance to Defense and Aviation and Chemical Defense of the USSR) at 14. This organization provided military-related training in shooting, radio operation, driving, chemical defense, parachuting, glider-flying, and other skills. Hundreds of thousands made parachute jumps, as parachuting became a national craze. The OSOAVIAHIM offered a diversion for youths; there was little else to do and it was paid for by the government. The organization claimed 13 million members in 1941. While the quality of pre-military instruction in both schools and the OSOAVIAHIM may have been patchy, it did help the mobilization effort and provided some degree of preparation. The USSR was able to field large numbers of parachute units, radio operators (with a basic knowledge of Morse code), qualified vehicle drivers, and experienced shooters.

Conscription training

In peacetime training would last six months to a year, but during the war it was reduced to weeks, based on whatever time was available. Training conditions were difficult for instructors and troops. Weapons, ammunition, technical equipment, ranges, and simple training aids were in short supply. Many of the instructors were unskilled and not always familiar with their subjects. Some instructors were reservists and not conversant with the newer weapons and tactics.

The training day began with reveille between 0500 and 0600hrs. The recruits dressed and cleaned up to rush though a quick breakfast. Training lasted 10–12 hours six days a week. Sunday was off, but far from a free day – quarters were cleaned, any weapons and equipment were maintained, and there were lessons to study. There was, of course, no church call. There were short hourly breaks throughout the day and an hour for lunch. Dinner was eaten after training was completed. In the evenings boots and equipment were cleaned and prepared for the next day. The study of manuals might be required or there could be political indoctrination lectures, films, and discussions.

In the first days of training the military regulations were read to the recruits and motivational/propaganda talks given. Training was unimaginative for the most part, although the few combat veterans (most recent veterans were at the front) would present more practical instruction, especially in small-unit tactics. Instruction was repetitive and often learned only by rote and unthinking reception. This system was complicated by the limited vocabulary of many recruits, the complicated Russian military vocabulary, and poor, or lack of, comprehension of Russian by some troops. Much of the instruction was presented by lecture, often merely read from the manual. The recruits sat on the ground, weather permitting. There were few if any classrooms available. In the snow or rain the troops would stand at attention in formation as the lecture was presented. On hot days when the troops began to nod off they would also be stood at attention.

Much time was first spent on the drill field learning how to march in formation, conduct facing movements, and drill with the rifle (often with sticks as substitutes). The recruits learned to move as a unit and to understand the importance of paying attention to commands. It was here that non-Russian speakers learned the words of command, often by mimicking the actions of others, reinforced by shouts, punches, and kicks. They also dug, with their little entrenching tools, fighting positions, trenches, drainage ditches, and dugout shelters. Exposure to the weather and hard work conditioned them mentally and physically. Time permitting, in the winter they might receive ski and snowshoe training, although this was more often done within units.

Recruits took the Military Oath of the Red Army after they demonstrated an understanding of the regulations regarding discipline and of the oath's significance, but not later than two months after assignment to a unit. This was scheduled for a Sunday and regarded as a unit holiday, with the entire unit paraded in full uniform and colors. Each man swore the oath individually, signed the document, and the date was entered in his Red Army Pass. The oath ran as follows:

I, _____, a citizen of the Union of the Soviet Socialist Republics, entering into the ranks of the Red Army of Workers and Peasants, take this oath and solemnly promise to be an honest, brave, disciplined, vigilant fighter, staunchly to protect military and state secrets, and unquestioningly to obey all military regulations and orders of commanders and superiors.

I promise conscientiously to study military affairs, in every way to protect military and state property, and to my last breath to be faithful to the people, the Soviet Motherland, and the Workers-Peasants' Government.

I am always prepared on order of the Workers and Peasants' Government to rise to the defense of my Motherland, the Union of Soviet Socialist Republics; and as a fighting man of the Red Army of Workers and Peasants, I promise to defend it bravely, skillfully, with dignity and honor, sparing neither my blood nor my life itself for the achievement of total victory over our enemies.

If by evil intent I should violate this, my solemn oath, then let the severe punishment of Soviet law and the total hatred and contempt of the working classes befall me.

Tactical lessons and training manuals

The Red Army's 1936 infantry tactics manual was simplistic and straightforward. The November 1942 manual, incorporating lessons learned, remained uncomplicated. The following discussion of tactics is based on the 1942 manual. The manual's simplicity was just as well, considering the inexperience of leaders and troops. Small-unit movement and battle formations, and the layout of defensive positions, were simply described and kept to a minimum of variants that were

It is often claimed that Red Army troops could not perform any other jobs but their own. Even though they may not have been initially trained on other platoon weapons, they often used them the field. Here a section commander familiarizes his men with the 7.62mm DP machine gun. (Nik Cornish Collection Y43)

relatively easy for inexperienced soldiers and commanders to visualize and comprehend. They were also easy to control and shift from one formation to another. The basic principles of these formations, tactics, and organization applied to all echelons up through the regiment.

The infantry manual spelled out the responsibilities of a soldier. In the West military manuals served as guidelines to be modified as the situation warranted. In the Red Army manuals had the force of law and infractions of the manual were punishable offenses. According to the manual:

Every soldier must:
- carry out without disagreement, precisely and quickly all orders and instructions of his commander;
- learn his combat mission and that of his section and platoon;
- possess complete knowledge of his weapons, maintain his mastery, and their permanent readiness;
- know his place in the battle formation from which he can carry out the commands and instructions of his commander, maintain constant coordination with his commander and neighboring soldiers;
- strive for mutual aid; constantly support his comrades with fire, bayonet, grenades, entrenching tool, and by personal example; protect and cover the commander in battle;
- in battle shoot carefully and accurately, report to the commander when he has expended half his ammunition so that it can be replenished; remove ammunition and grenades from the dead and wounded, and collect ammunition found on the battlefield;
- bring ammunition whenever returning from the rear;
- at all halts dig in and camouflage;
- continuously observe the battlefield, neighboring units, the sky, and report all observations to the commander;
- if the commander becomes a casualty take command of the section and continue the battle;
- if separated from his section join the next section and continue the battle;
- if wounded bandage himself and continue the battle; he is allowed to go to the aid station only with approval of the commander and must take with him his weapon and cartridge belt (magazines); if he cannot go on he crawls to cover with his weapon and awaits a medic.

Soldiers were further admonished that "It is forbidden to leave the battlefield to escort the wounded" and "Every soldier must hate the enemy, maintain military secrecy, be vigilant, unmask spies and saboteurs, and relentlessly act against traitors to the Motherland." Furthermore, "Nothing, including the threat of death, allows a soldier of the Red Army to surrender or in any way reveal a military secret." Just about anything to do with the military was secret in the security-paranoid USSR.

Weapons training
Weapons training was often limited owing to arms and ammunition shortages. Firing ranges were not always available. Operator training

and maintenance was conducted with a few shared weapons. "Dry firing" – without ammunition – to learn weapon operation, sighting, and firing positions was conducted. Many soldiers were fortunate to fire just 3–5 rounds. When issued a weapon they usually went into combat without firing it or zeroing its sight. As with learning tactics and how to survive on the battlefield, those living through their first battles became proficient with their weapons and often learned how to operate all of those in their unit.

More care was given to machine-gun training, but, again, too often only a few guns were available and the operators might not fire any live rounds during training. Antitank riflemen received careful instruction oriented to choosing firing positions and targeting vulnerable points on tanks. Mortar training was frequently poor because of the scarcity of ammunition and the average conscript's difficulty in understanding the complexities of indirect, unobserved fire and the mortar's intricate sight. Even officers had difficulty learning the weapon's complexities in their rushed training. Crews did gain proficiency in combat, however, making the mortar a valuable weapon.

Other training provided to rifle troops was typical of any other army: bayonet, fire against aircraft, actions against tanks, scouting, observing and reporting information, duties in outposts, messenger duties, chemical defense, guard duty, field sanitation, first-aid, camouflage, field fortifications, and breaching obstacles. Land navigation and map reading were something only sergeants and commanders were taught.

Recruits undergo rifle training, despite there being no uniforms issued. Presenting instruction on the Mosin-Nagant M1891/30 rifle is a senior lieutenant. Lecture was the standard means of presenting instruction, and the troops stand at attention to keep them from dozing off. (Nik Cornish Collection T2)

Organization and attack formations of a rifle regiment

The *vzvod* (rifle platoon) had a four-man headquarters and four nine-man *otdyeleniye* (rifle sections) for a total of 40 men. Previously 11-man sections had been fielded for a strength of 48 men. The platoon had two "light" or Type A sections with one light machine gun apiece and two "heavy" or Type B sections with two guns each. Both were the same strength, the number of riflemen being different. Owing to shortages there might be only one machine gun per section. With losses platoons typically fielded three or even just two sections and the remaining machine guns were more or less evenly allocated between 20–30 men. The section commander had a rifle, but by 1943 he more commonly had a submachine gun, and there might be two or three more submachine guns assigned to each section, including to the assistant machine gunner.

The section fell in to the left of the section commander, a junior sergeant, who signaled this by standing at attention with his left arm outstretched horizontally to his side. The rest of the section fell in at arm intervals. In training they fell in by height, but in an organized fully trained section it was in a specific order according to duties from the left of the section commander: machine gunner, assistant machine gunner, second machine gun crew if assigned, observer/guide, and the riflemen. The last man in the file, the "closing man," was the most dependable rifleman, who brought up the rear, ensuring no one lagged behind. The observer/guide, a corporal, was the assistant section commander, aiding with control. The platoon would fall in with its 2–4 sections in parallel ranks. The platoon commander was centered in the front, the deputy platoon commander (sergeant) to the rear, and the two platoon messengers fell in at the end of sections with fewer men. The messengers may have relayed orders to section commanders, but their primary responsibility was to relay information to the company commander, who would send orders back with them or use his own messengers.

The basic section movement formation was the single-file column or "chain." The men were arranged in the same way as when they fell in, with the section commander at the head of the file. There were no wedge (inverted "V"), echeloned, or more complex movement formations. The column was easy to control, was relatively fast moving – each man did not have to break his own trail as in dispersed formations, something especially useful in dense vegetation or deep snow – was the quietest at night and in thick vegetation for the same reason, and helped keep men from becoming separated. The only variant of the column was the skirmish column with the men positioned at extended intervals, up to eight paces depending on visibility, rather than one or two paces.

There was only one attack formation, the skirmish line. Moving in a column, the section commander ordered "Halt," and the men assumed the prone position. The section commander would then order, "By the center skirmish line," or "Skirmish line to the left (right)." "By the center" meant the machine-gun crew moved to the right of the section commander and the observer/guide to the left. If there was a second machine-gun crew it would move to the left and the observer/guide to its left. The assistant gunner was always to the gunner's right. Riflemen would then alternate moving to the right and left after the observer/guide until all were on line. This would be accomplished all at once at the run and required only seconds – a soldier did not wait for the man in front to move

Rifle regiment, December 1942

Regimental Headquarters
- Headquarters Platoon
- Antiaircraft Platoon
  3 x 12.7mm DShK-38 MG
- Horse Reconnaissance Platoon
- Foot Reconnaissance Platoon
- Sapper Platoon
- Chemical Defense Platoon

Rifle Battalion (x3)
- Battalion Headquarters
- Signal Platoon
- Rifle Company (x3)
  12 x DP MG, 1 x PM-10 MG, 2 x 50mm mortar
- Machine Gun Company
  9 x PM-10 MG
- Mortar Company
  9 x 82mm mortar
- Antitank Gun Platoon
  2 x 45mm AT gun
- Antitank Rifle Platoon
  3 x 14.5mm AT rifle
- Medical Platoon
- Battalion Trains

Submachine Gun Company

Regimental Gun Battery
  4 x 76mm gun

Mortar Battery
  7 x 120mm mortar

Antitank Gun Battery
  6 x 45mm AT gun

Antitank Rifle Company
  27 x 14.5mm AT rifle

Signal Company

Transport Company

Medical Company

Veterinary Hospital

Weapons Repair Workshop

Regimental Trains

before moving himself. "Skirmish line to the left (right)" saw the men swinging out to the left (right) of the section commander, remaining in their same order. "Skirmish line to the left" resulted in the section commander being on the right end of the line and the left end for "skirmish line right." The interval between individuals was 6–8 paces.

Platoons moved and attacked in the same formations. A platoon skirmish line occupied about a 100-yard front with four sections on line. The only complex formation was the platoon rhomboid (diamond) with one section forward, two some distance to the rear and separated by almost 100 yards, and one to the rear with the platoon command group forward of the rear section and roughly between the flanking sections. This formation allowed sections to be maneuvered to outflank an enemy position or respond to an enemy surprise attack.

The key difference between Soviet section and platoon tactics and those of the Germans (and Western Allies) was that there was no fire and maneuver or leap-frogging of sections whereby one unit covered those advancing. Sections and platoons assaulted as a body. Other platoons might provide covering fire along with supporting fire from crew-served weapons, but the assault platoons simply advanced as one.

Platoons and sections could advance at a walk, run, move in short bounds from cover to cover, or low-crawl depending on the situation, enemy fire, and available cover. This manner of movement was specified when the attack order was given. The section commander and observer/guide ensured the men were generally aligned, but the line was not expected to be perfectly dressed – it could be staggered. If enemy fire was heavy and concealment existed, the unit infiltrated or "seeped" into the enemy position.

When the platoon had closed in and was able to make its final assault rush, the troops were ordered to ensure that weapons were fully loaded and grenades prepared. On the order, *Na shturm, marshch!* (Assault, march!), they rose as a body and advanced at a run without bunching up or halting. Within 40–50 yards of the enemy positions they shouted the Russian battle cry, a deep drawn out *Urra!*, pronounced "oo-rah," which translates as "Hurrah!" and is thought to come from the Turkish word for "kill."[1] They fired on the move and, when within range of enemy positions, threw grenades. They closed in rapidly for *blizhnii boi* (close combat) with point-blank fire, bayonets, weapon butts, entrenching tools, and fists.

Once the objective was seized the troops mopped up, ensuring dugouts and fighting positions were cleared. Communications trenches, gullies, and other routes leading into the positions were secured and covered, and also exploited to continue the advance into the enemy's flanks and rear. The troops were to align themselves with only the most advanced men and be prepared to repel enemy counterattacks.

Training in section and platoon movement and assault formations began on an open field where the troops could see what was going on and where everyone was supposed to be. Then they moved to fields of high grass or scattered brush, and finally to a forest.

Positions were well camouflaged. It is said that peasants and others who lived in the country excelled at camouflage, making it appear natural and blending it into surrounding terrain. Soldiers from cities were less skillful. Obstacles and positions were often emplaced on reverse slopes to conceal them from ground observation and direct fire, although this location silhouetted an attacking soldier against the sky as he crested the high ground. Positions were also emplaced within forests and villages rather than on the edges. Decoy positions were common.

The Soviet soldier was renowned for withholding fire until the Germans were at close range. At the beginning of the war Soviet doctrine called for weapons to engage the enemy at maximum range, but it was found more effective to "ambush" him with a surprise burst from all weapons within optimum range from multiple directions. Reserve (alternate) firing positions were prepared for crew-served weapons, not only to occupy when the primary positions became untenable, but to mislead the enemy as to the location and numbers of weapons by constantly shifting positions. Supplementary positions were prepared to allow weapons to cover other sectors – flanks and rear.

Training was often cut short. Troops were needed at the front to organize new units or rebuild battered formations. Such events frequently occurred without warning. Troops would be ordered to return to their quarters, pack their gear, and march to the nearest railroad station, sometimes without weapons. Weapons and ammunition would be issued at a railhead. There were actually incidents as depicted in the motion picture *Enemy at the Gates* (2001), when every other man was handed a rifle and a few clips, and the rest told to pick up weapons from the fallen.

Training units sent to the front in an emergency may have actually fought as units in some instances, with unfamiliar officers assigned directly from academies. Conversely, they might have been broken up into subunits to replace other units destroyed in battle. The soldiers could also be assigned as individual replacements. More often, trained replacements were sent to the front in "march units" as individual replacements to be assigned to engaged units, units in reserve, or units being reconstituted after prolonged action.

---

1. The cry had been in use since at least the time of Peter the Great, around 1700. The Prussians adopted the same battle cry after hearing it from the Russians during the 1756–63 Seven Years' War and it continued to be used by the Germans. The Russian version was said to be deeper and more mournful than the German, and German veterans claim its memory still chills them.

Russian combat commands	
Russian	**English**
Smirno	Attention
Marshch	March
Stoi	Halt
Vystranvat v sherengu	Form line
V tsep	Skirmish line
Napravo	Right
Nalevo	Left
Ogon	Fire
Odinochnyi ogon	Free fire
Na boem	To battle (an alert for action)
Na shturm	To the assault
Bezopasnyi	[At a] run
Prekray strel'bu	Cease fire
Tyl'	Rear (withdraw)

APPEARANCE

The average Slav was 5ft 6in., as were most of the USSR's ethnic minorities. There were blonde, brown, and red heads, but by far most had black hair and brown eyes. One contemporary description described "Great Russians" as "possessing eyes ranging from dark to light, fair to dark complexion, greater than average stature, moderate brachycephaly [short-headedness], and well-proportioned and well-developed limbs." Hair was generally kept clipped very short all around. Even if worn an inch or so long on the top, the sides were clipped. This was for sanitation reasons – it made hair less vulnerable to head lice and easier to wash. Short-trimmed mustaches were seen, but were quite rare. Long mustaches were common among Cossacks.

Red Army uniforms were simple and functional, with little in the way of insignia (the traditional Russian rank system had been abandoned). The insignia system was dictated by the 1935 *Prikaz* 176 regulations (traditional rank titles were not reintroduced until this year), and general ranks were restored in May 1940. Previously, position titles were used. The new rank titles and insignia were based on those of the Russian Empire, although they underwent some modifications. In an effort to improve morale, in 1943 new regulations were issued, *Prakaz* 25, reestablishing traditional insignia and titles, provided for other insignia, and new uniform components. Gold braid was even requested through Lend-Lease, but rejected by the US.

There was no unit identification, only branch of service devices and colored piping worn on rank shoulder straps and collar tabs. The infantry used raspberry piping, but had no branch insignia as other branches. Loyalty was to the Party and State, not to a unit. Personal awards for valor, merit, and service were increased and worn on the uniform, even in combat.

Even before the 1943 reforms the Soviet soldier wore traditional Russian-style *zashchitniy tsvet* uniforms of light olive-brown or olive-drab.

An officer reads instructions during a guard mount. The double-breasted greatcoats were made of shoddy wool, as can be seen in the appearance of these soldiers' coats. Some officers wore lined black or dark-brown leather jackets as here. (Nik Cornish Collection B75)

Photographs, however, depict soldiers wearing uniforms ranging across tans, browns, greens, and grays, all within the same unit and with mismatched tunics and trousers. From 1944 uniforms were a darker olive-green shade. Different models of uniform were sometimes worn within the same unit. Newly raised units and units sent to the rear for rebuilding would be outfitted with new uniform issues. Soldiers considered their uniforms to be comfortable and often of better quality than their civilian clothes.

Headgear included the *pilotka* (side cap), the distinctive overseas-type field cap, often worn jauntily canted down to the right ear. It bore an olive-green star with a raised hammer and sickle, but could be replaced by an enameled red star bearing a gold hammer and sickle. Officers were issued a *shelm* or *budionovka* (peaked cap), a round service cap with a black visor. The cap band, with a red enameled metal star, and the crown edge piping were in the branch color.

The olive-drab steel helmet was to be worn in combat, sometimes with a solid or outlined red star painted on the front. They might be whitewashed in winter or white cloth covers were fabricated. Steel helmets offered no protection from the cold and could even cause frostbite on the tops of ears – soldiers sometimes removed the liner so it could be worn over the fur cap. Commanders often had problems enforcing the wear of helmets as soldiers considered helmets unmanly and so fines and penalties had to be imposed. In the early days helmets were not available to many units and some still lacked them in 1945.

The 1936 uniform consisted of the *gymnastiorka* (tunic) based on the traditional peasant's blouse. The loose-fitting pullover had a front opening extending halfway down the chest. Its patch-type breast pockets had buttoned flaps and it had a stand-and-fall collar, usually worn buttoned closed. Collar and front opening buttons were concealed. Olive-green metal rank insignia were worn on elongated collar tabs that were the same color as the uniform. Officers usually had branch-color piped tabs. The olive-green pocket flap buttons were exposed, but might

The 1942 uniform had a standing collar and rank was worn on shoulder straps. The buttons were removable and for parade and walking-out wear the green buttons would be replaced by brass. The man to the left is armed with a 7.62mm PPS-43 submachine gun.

Soviet steel helmets
The most common helmet through the war was the SSh-40 (*Stalshlyem* – steel hat), similar in shape to the American M1 and Italian M33 helmets. There was also a lesser used SSh-39 of similar design, the differences being the internal padding and that the SSh-39 had three rivets while the SSh-40 had six. The earlier Kaska-36 helmet and the SSh-39 remained in production into 1941. (The Kaska-36 saw diminishing use through the war.) The SSh-39 was produced by three factories, two of which were in Stalingrad, which explains why SSh-40 production was pursued elsewhere. It had a distinctively long visor, flared ear protectors, and a small crest on the crown to deflect saber blows, an outdated feature. It was known as the *Khalkingolka*, owing to its first use in action at Khalkin Gol in Siberia against the Japanese in 1938. Some Kaska-28 helmets, copies of the French M1915 Adrian helmet, were still in use early in the war. Internal helmet padding liners might be leather or fabric. Brown leather and web chin straps were used. The Kaska-36 and SSh-39 were issued in four sizes (1–4, 4 being the largest). The SSh-40 was issued in sizes 1–3.

be replaced by brass buttons, especially on officers' tunics. The 1943 field uniform was similar to the 1936, but had a more traditional standing collar, and rank was displayed on shoulder straps. A white tack-stitched collar liner was used, but often disappeared during field duty. It had three front-opening and two collar buttons, olive-green or brass. The breast pockets were concealed, but with single-buttoned flaps. Rank was displayed on the shoulder straps. The *sharovari* (trousers) were semi-breeches, loose-fitting around the thighs and tight at the ankles with tie tapes. The field uniform was cotton for summer wear, which faded considerably, and wool for winter. Late in the war the United States provided high-quality uniforms through Lend-Lease.

The 1936 uniform had a stand-and-fall collar, normally with collar tabs. The center man is armed with a 7.62mm PPSh-41 submachine gun; note the 71-round drum magazine pouch on his belt. The man to the left has an F-1 "lemon" fragmentation grenade on his belt. (Nik Cornish Collection K64)

Black leather ankle-high boots were standard issue for the summer months. These were worn with tan or olive-drab puttees. In the winter high-top black leather marching boots – termed *govnodavy* (shit-tramper) – were issued. In reality either boot might be worn in any season. Marching boots were issued a size larger so two or more layers of footwraps could protect the feet. Boots would also be lined with newspaper, straw, or cloth in the winter. *Portyanki* (footwraps) – cotton or wool rectangles – were traditional and preferred by many old soldiers. They cost less than socks and did not wear out as fast. Footwrap cloth was issued in bolts and soldiers cut the wraps to size. Officers were sometimes issued socks and socks might be sent by a soldier's family. German footwear was commonly looted.

The brownish-gray wool *shinel* (greatcoat) completed the uniform; its traditional color was effective camouflage in winter woods against brownish-gray tree trunks and mist, although some were olive-drab. It was carried in all but the hottest summer months. The Soviet soldier was not issued blankets or sleeping bags; his greatcoat was meant to suffice. Of course, commandeered civilian and captured German blankets were valued.

Two officers, one seated in the center (captain) and the other standing to the right rear (senior lieutenant), chat with their soldiers. The shaven-headed man to the right is a sergeant major. They wear the 1936 uniform and collar rank insignia. (Nik Cornish Collection L88)

The *plasch palatkas* (shelter-cape) was a roughly triangular-shaped waterproof multiuse item. A tape and button at the base of the hood fastened around the neck and held the cape in place when worn over the shoulders. On the lower center of the back was a wooden toggle to which the lower corner grommet was attached to keep it off the ground. The grommets were leather-reinforced. As a shelter, the shelter-cape could be rigged as a lean-to or ground-cloth, or the soldier could roll up in it. Two could be laced together with a cord through the grommets, but the ends were open. A cramped six-man tent could be rigged with two laced-together capes on either side and one on each end. As a bedroll it was rolled in a U-shape with the greatcoat inside and the ends secured by a leather strap or cord. Shelter-capes were usually light olive-green, gray-green, or dark tan. The similar officer's *plasch nikidka* could not be used as a shelter-half; it had arm slits in the sides, an adjustable neck tape, and buttons to hold the hood in place when not used.

The brutal Russian winter demanded protective clothing. Even though the Red Army was intimately familiar with the winter, in the early stages of the war it was not always well prepared, often due to production shortfalls. It was, for example, impossible to produce sufficient clothing for issue in the winter of 1941/42. The invasion took the logistics system by surprise and it was unable to issue standard uniforms and equipment to the rapidly expanding army and prepare for the winter, which imposed itself less than five months after the Germans attacked.

Enlisted men's uniform issue		
Uniform Components	Summer	Winter
cap	1 field cap	1 fur cap
greatcoat	1 year-round	
toque		1
sheepskin coat		1
shelter-cape	1 year-round	
tunic, field	2 cotton	1 wool
tunic, padded		1
trousers, field	2 pr cotton	1 pr wool
trousers, padded		1 pr
undershirt	2 year-round	
underdrawers	3 pr year-round	
undershirt, warm		1
underdrawers, warm		1 pr
footwraps	3 pr cotton	2 pr wool
puttee	1 pr	
ankle boots	1 pr	
high boots		1 pr
felt boots w/insoles		1 pr
mittens		1 pr
towel	2 year-round	
handkerchief	3 year-round	

A rifleman digs a hasty fighting position in a mustard-gas contaminated area. He wears a BN gas mask, rubberized protective over-boots and gloves, and lies on a shelter-cape (the hood is seen beside his knee). Much emphasis was placed on chemical defense prior to the war.

Cold weather clothing was inadequate during the Winter War in Finland and changes were only just being implemented.

The old-type bluntly pointed *budionovka* or *vki* (wool cap) had a fold-up woolen ear and neck flap and a small visor. It proved ineffective in Finland's severe cold, but was still being issued. The 1940 *shapka-ushanka* (fur cap) had a fur-lined brownish-gray wool crown, fold-up visor, and ear flaps that tied over the top when not needed. The visor and ear flaps were fur-covered and known as "fish fur caps," as the artificial fur bore no resemblance to that of any animal.

The winter uniform consisted of a *telogreika* (padded jacket) and *vatnie sharovari* (padded trousers) worn over the wool winter field uniform. They were sewn with vertical tubes filled with cotton batting. The *telogreika* lacked breast pockets, had a full-length front opening secured by loops and toggles or buttons, and could have a short standing collar or an earlier stand-and-fall-type. Other issue winter clothing included a *polushubok* (sheepskin jacket), *shuba* (sheepskin coat), and *sakui* (sealskin coveralls). There were shortages throughout the war and much use was made of civilian and German winter clothing. White cotton and wool long *portyanki* (underwear) were issued along with knitted wool *sviter* (sweaters), *rukavitsa* (mittens); and knitted, canvas, and leather

Snipers move into position amid the ruins of a city. Snow-camouflage suits were available to many units with the onset of winter. The Germans were ill prepared in this regard.

Rifle troops clad in the padded winter uniform. The man to the left is armed with a 7.62mm SVT-40 semi-automatic rifle. The others have various German weapons. The man in the center with the black cap has a 7.9mm Kar 98k carbine and the second from the left a World War I Kar 98a carbine. (Nik Cornish Collection T16)

perchatka (gloves) with fur lining. Women knitted millions of scarves and socks and these were distributed to troops by the Party.

For very cold weather high-top 0.25in.-thick compressed gray felt boots – *valenki* – were issued and proved popular, but soaked through and disintegrated in the spring snowmelt. Civilian equivalents were often commandeered. During the rainy spring and autumn, high-topped *kirozoviy sapogi* – waterproof canvas boots with leather soles – were sometimes issued.

In the early days of the war it was not uncommon for troops to go into combat wearing civilian clothes, Western-style business suits with vests, and worker's uniforms with round caps. Gulag convicts went into combat wearing their black uniforms.

WEAPONS AND EQUIPMENT

Weapons

Soviet infantry weapons were known for their simplicity, ruggedness, and general reliability. The average soldier had very little in the way of technical knowledge. Factory workers and farmhands used only simple tools, often manual. Equipment operators were taught to operate one type of machine or were responsible for one function on an assembly line. Therefore, weapons needed to be simple to operate and maintain. Reliability was essential, not only for the obvious reason – effective function in combat – but also to endure the climate extremes and the poor logistics that could not be counted on to provide spare parts and repairs. The Soviet soldier would not hesitate to criticize an ineffective weapon, which he would call a *pukalka* (wind-emitter).

It was not until the 1890s that Russia began developing its own weapons, although foreign-designed weapons or weapons borrowing

Red Army rank titles	
Russian	**English**
Krasnoarmeets	Red Army man (private)
Yefrejtor	corporal
Mladshiy Sergant	junior sergeant
Sergant	sergeant
Starshii Sergant	senior sergeant
Starshina	sergeant major
Mladshiy Lejtenant	junior lieutenant
Lejtenant	lieutenant
Starshiy Lejtenant	senior lieutenant
Kapitan	captain
Major	major
Podpolkovnik	lieutenant colonel
Polkovnik	colonel
General-Major	general-major
General-Lejtenant	general-lieutenant
General-Polkovnik	general-colonel
General Armii	army general
*Marshal**	marshal
*Glavniy Marshal**	major marshal
Marshal Sovetkogo Soyuza	marshal of the Soviet Union

*Followed by: *Aviatsii* (Aviation), *Artillerii* (Artillery), *Bronetankovykh Vojsk* (Armored Troops), *Vojsk Svyazi* (Signals Troops), *Inzhenernykh Vojsk* (Engineer Troops).

The ranks of Guards unit personnel were preceded by *Gvardiya* (Guards).

Snipers climb a riverbank as they search for good firing positions. Snipers operated in pairs, covering the same sector from nearby positions or one firing and the other spotting. They are armed with specially selected 7.62mm Mosin-Nagant M1891/30 *snaiperskaya* (sniper rifles) with turn-down bolt handles and telescope mounts, here with the 4x PE. (Nik Cornish Collection L63)

foreign influence were still in use in the Great Patriotic War. Most infantry weapons at the war's beginning were adequate and by 1943 numerous new and more effective weapons were being fielded.

For most soldiers the rifle was the most complex piece of machinery they had ever dealt with – for a farmhand experienced in handling picks, shovels, hoes, and sickles, the bolt-action Mosin-Nagant 7.62mm M1891/30 rifle was advanced technology. The M1891/30 remained the standard infantry rifle through the war and was known to soldiers as the *vintovka Mosina* (Mosin rifle) or by an old term, *trechlineynaja* (three-line).[2] For the era it was a comparatively long rifle being 48.5in. long, 5in. longer than the German Kar 98k carbine. While rugged and reliable, its bolt was overly complex and required good cleaning. The rifleman also considered his weapon heavy at 8.75lb – with its web sling and bayonet another pound was added. The 17in.-long M1891 cruciform *shtik* (spike bayonet) had a locking socket that fitted around the foresight. It also had a screwdriver-type flat tip and could be used as such. The bayonet was habitually carried fixed to the rifle and seldom were scabbards issued. (Prior to and early in the war bayonet scabbards were issued to some units. These were simple tubular leather or canvas sheaths.)

When the soldier was in rear areas, traveling in trucks or trains, or inside restricted fortifications, the bayonet was reversed with the blade running down the fore-end. It was usually a tight fit and difficult to remove and attach. On early production rifles, the fitting often loosened.

The Mosin's shooting qualities were reasonable. The rear sight was graduated from 100–2,000m and was ill-suited for a fine degree of accuracy, but its realistic combat range was about 400 yards. The bolt-action was fairly smooth and quick to operate, but the safety was stiff. It was operated by rotating the knob on the end of the bolt to the right to lock it on safe. If wet and then frozen it could be difficult to unlock – soldiers were taught to urinate on it for an immediate thaw-out. The rifle's internal magazine was loaded with a five-round charging clip, which was inserted into slots in the rear of the receiver and the rounds

2. The term was based on an old system of measurement in which "one-line" equaled 0.10in. "Three-line" equaled 0.33in. or .30-cal. (7.62mm).

pushed down into the magazine with the thumb. When the bolt was closed, a round would be chambered, but the rounds could be depressed into the magazine with the thumb and the bolt closed over the round. A charger was not necessary, as rounds could be inserted individually into the magazine. A rifleman could crack off 8–10 aimed rounds a minute with reloading.

Two carbine versions of the Mosin were issued to engineers, artillerymen, cavalrymen, signalmen, and other auxiliary troops. By 1943 they were also being issued to some infantry units fighting in cities, notably Stalingrad, to provide a more manageable weapon in confined spaces. The M1938 was only 40in. long, weighed 7.62lb, and had a rear sight graduated for only 100–1,000m. A bayonet could not be fitted as it was of little use to cavalrymen and support troops. The M1944 was identical, but had a permanently attached 12.25in.-long folding spike bayonet, which folded along the right side. Prototypes of this carbine were issued in Stalingrad in late 1943. The carbines were noted for their hard recoil owing to their short barrels.

The USSR was one of the first nations to adopt a semi-automatic rifle on a large scale. Early efforts were too flimsy, complex, and expensive. This was especially true of the Tokarev 7.62mm SVT-38 rifle (SVT – Samozaryadnaya Vintovka Tokareva – Self-loading Rifle Tokarev). It was dropped in 1940, although it was pressed into service after the German invasion. The SVT-40 was a bit more robust, but still considered too fragile for general combat use. Prior to the war a few units were fully armed with the SVT-40, but they were destroyed in combat and the remaining rifles distributed piecemeal to Mosin-armed units. They may have been given to selected soldiers or sergeants.

The SVT-40 was 48.1in. long making it almost as long as the Mosin, because it had a muzzle break. It weighed 8.59lb without its detachable ten-round magazine. It had a conventional 9.5in. blade bayonet with a metal scabbard. A man armed with an SVT-40 usually carried one spare magazine in a leather pouch and routinely reloaded the magazine in the rifle using two five-round charger clips. A good shooter could fire and reload about 40 rounds per minute (rpm), if he had four ten-round magazines. If he had to reload with chargers he might get off 20–25rpm. Firepower was not significantly increased, with just a few SVTs distributed to a rifle platoon.

A key weapon of the rifle section was its one or two 7.62mm Degtyarev DP light machine guns (DP – *Degtyaryova Pakhotnyi* – Degtyarev Infantry) adopted in 1928. The bipod-mounted DP could be fired from the ground or from the underarm or hip position when advancing. It was provided

A patrol sets out from a unit command post. The man in the lower right strips a clip of rounds into his Mosin-Nagant M1938 carbine. The troops wear the padded *telogreika* (winter uniform jacket).

A greatcoat-clad DP machine-gun crew fires on a German-occupied apartment block. The gunner has additional pan magazines in his simple backpack. The assistant is armed with a Mosin-Nagant M1944 carbine with its integral bayonet folded. The brownish-gray greatcoat blended in well within cities.

A PM-10 Maxim machine-gun crew hammer out rounds. The riveted fabric belts were issued to the crew, who had to load the belt with loose cartridges. Empty belts were never discarded. Note that the Sokolov mount's shield and barrel jacket have been whitewashed. (Nik Cornish Collection L40)

with a 47-round pan magazine, resulting in its being called the *proigryvatel'* (record-player). It weighed 26.3lb loaded and was 50in. long. It could hammer out 500–600rpm. The DP was about the same weight, length, and bulk as the 7.9mm MG34, the German squad automatic weapon, but the MG34 was a belt-fed weapon with a quick-change barrel, was more rugged, and put out 800–900rpm. Fired in short bursts, the DP had a practical rate of fire of about 80rpm, but was considered a bit fragile and its operating spring was coiled around the under-barrel operating rod, which resulted in the spring heating up and distorting, causing malfunctions. The DP was redesigned and the DPM (*Degtyaryova Pakhotnyi Modernizirovaiiyy* – Degtyarev Infantry Modernized) was fielded in 1944. The recoil spring was relocated to a tubular housing protruding from the rear of the receiver, the safety lever was improved, a pistol grip added, and the bipod fitting strengthened and redesigned so the gun could be set up on uneven ground. To make up for shortages, DT (*Degtyaryova Tankovyi*) tank machine guns were adapted to infantry use. The DT had a ratchet-type telescoping steel butt stock, pistol grip, and 60-round pan magazine. In the infantry role a bipod was attached to the firing port adapter ring and iron sights added. The DT was widely used in the infantry role and reported to be popular due to the magazine capacity. (The magazines were not interchangeable between the DP/DPM and DT/DTM.) The DTM, incorporating similar improvements as the DPM, was also modified to an infantry machine gun.

Only small numbers of the Degtyarev 7.62mm PPD-34/38 and PPD-40 submachine guns were available at the war's beginning. The numbers increased in 1943 and by 1944 one in four riflemen was so armed. The most common, and practically a symbol of the Red Army, was the 7.62mm PPSh-41 (PPSh – *Pistolet-Pulemet Shpagina* – Pistol-Automatic Shpagin). Also known as the *peh-peh-shah* or *balalaika*, the PPSh-41 was a rugged and reliable weapon, being only 33.15in. long, but heavy at 12lb with a loaded 71-round drum magazine. The underpowered pistol round was its major deficiency, as was the magazine, which was heavy, slow and difficult to load, expensive, easily damaged, and rattled. In 1944 a more reliable curved 35-round magazine issued with the PPS-43 (see below) became available for the PPSh-41 and reduced the loaded weight to 9.26lb. Its rate of fire was unnecessarily high at 700–900 rpm. The PPSh-41 required an exceedingly heavy 20–25lb trigger pull.

A less frequently used submachine gun was the PPS-43 (*Pistolet-Pulemet Sudarev* – Pistol-Automatic Sudarev). It was largely made of stampings and had a folding steel stock: with the stock extended the gun was 32.72in. long, folded it was 24.25in. long. It weighed 7.98lb with its loaded 35-round magazine and fired at a more practical 650rpm.

Handguns were mainly issued to officers, but many company officers armed themselves with submachine guns. Most weapons crewmen were issued carbines or submachine guns. It was common for the gunner himself to be armed with only his primary weapon, especially if this was a machine gun. The Tokarev 7.62mm TT-33 was a compact pistol with an eight-round magazine and weighed 1.88lb. Wide use was also made of the obsolete Nagant 7.62mm M1895 double-action revolver. It has a unique means of sealing the gap between the cylinder and barrel. The mouth of the cartridge case protruded slightly beyond the cylinder (the bullet was completely recessed in the case). When cocked the cylinder cammed forward and the end of the case was set into the barrel. This system increased the velocity and range of the otherwise underpowered round. As the gun was of small caliber, the cylinder had seven chambers. The revolver weighed 1.65lb.

Hand grenades were widely used and included the F-1 fragmentation (known as the *limonka* – lemon), RG-42 fragmentation, and RGD-33 blast grenades, the latter with a slip-on fragmentation sleeve. *Ruchnaya Protivotankovoye Granata* (hand antitank grenade) types included the

A PM-10 Maxim is hand-carried forward at a more rapid rate than it could be dragged on its wheels over the rough ground. Removing the shield significantly reduced its weight. Examples are found with both fluted and smooth barrel jackets, the latter being of earlier production. The ammunition held a 250-round belt. (Nik Cornish Collection L42)

RPG-40, RPG-43, and RPG-6. Large numbers of German 6.6lb magnetic hollow-charge hand-mines were used. These represented such a threat that the Germans were forced to apply "anti-magnetic" plaster on their tanks and assault guns for protection from a hand-delivered weapon of their own making.

What the Russians called a *Butylka s goryuchej smes' yu* (lit. "bottle with flammable mixture") was seldom referred to as a *Molotov-kokteil* (Molotov cocktail) as it was not "politically correct" to make light of their leaders' names. Besides the usual Molotov cocktails made in the field with rag wicks, in 1940 the Soviets provided two "incendiary liquid kits" to ensure more reliable ignition: No.1 and the KS. These consisted of a sulfuric acid-based compound in two long paper-covered tubes attached to gasoline-filled vodka or cognac bottles by two rubber bands. When the bottles shattered upon impact the sulfuric acid reacted with and ignited the gasoline. Another method, when incendiary kits were not available, was to tie or tape a rag wad to the neck of a plugged bottle. The rag wad was soaked with gasoline from another bottle, lit, and the bottle thrown to ignite when shattered. This technique prevented the leakage problem.

Other than the antitank hand grenades and mostly ineffective antitank rifle grenades, there were no antitank weapons available to the rifle company. Two types of 14.5mm antitank rifles were often attached from battalion and regimental levels. Both bipod-mounted rifles were heavy and long, but could be broken down into two sections. The Degtyarov PTRD-41 was a single-shot bolt-action rifle, 78.74in. long and weighing 38lb. The Simonov PTRS-41 was semi-automatic with a five-round magazine and saw less service – it was expensive and complex. The 14.5mm armor-piercing incendiary round could penetrate 0.8in. of armor at 100 yards. Soon obsolete, the antitank rifles nevertheless remained in use, with tactics emphasizing side and rear attack as well as use against light armored fighting vehicles (AFVs), especially if used in large numbers. Some Lend-Lease antitank weapons were provided

Soviet ammunition
From left to right. The 14.5 x 114mm (the second number is the cartridge case length) armor-piercing incendiary round used in the PTRD-41 (*Protivotankovoye Ruzhyo Degtyaryova*) and PTRS-41 (*Protivotankovoye Ruzhyo Simonova*) antitank rifles. The Soviets used three different 7.62mm cartridges in the Great Patriotic War. The most common was the 7.62 x 54mm rimmed round used in rifles, carbines, and machine guns. Its performance was comparable to the German 7.9 x 57mm used in their counterpart weapons (pictured at the far right). The 7.62 x 38mm rimmed cartridge was used in Nagant M1895 revolvers. The bullet was seated completely inside the case, making it appear like an empty round. The little bottlenecked 7.62 x 25mm Tokarev was used in TT-33 pistols and Soviet submachine guns. It was an underpowered round with a light bullet that provided poor knockdown power and penetration. Ammunition was issued in galvanized metal cans opened by a key and strip. Rifle ammunition was clipped in chargers, but machine-gun rounds were loose, having to be belted or loaded into magazines by the crew. As often as not riflemen had to work with loose unclipped rounds for rifles.

by the United States and Britain: 2.36in. M1 bazookas, 0.55in. Boys antitank rifles, and PIAT Mk 1 antitank projectors.[3]

Each unit from section upwards possessed its own fire-support weapons. There were also additional supporting weapons at each echelon from company up that could be attached to selected subordinate units to augment their firepower, and/or were retained under the parent unit's control to allow the commander to reinforce or influence the combat capabilities of a subunit. The regiment especially was provided with a generous number of supporting weapons and rear service subunits, more so than any other nation's infantry regiment.

Rifle companies were provided with two, sometimes three, 50mm *Rotney Minomyot* (mortars): the RM-38, RM-39, RM-40, or RM-41. The first three were of the conventional Brandt design used by most countries, but each model was soon replaced owing to cost and manufacturing time. The RM-39 was also too heavy compared to the others. The RM-41 dispensed with the bipod to provide an even simpler weapon on a large base plate. Except for the 37.5lb RM-39, the mortars weighed 20–26.7lb and had a 870-yard range. They all fired the same high-explosive round, which was little more effective than a hand grenade. All models remained in use, but production ceased in early 1942, and they were withdrawn from service in 1944. Remaining rounds were converted to hand grenades.[4]

The spigot-type RM rifle grenade launcher firing the VGD-30 fragmentation and RPG-40 antitank grenades was used until phased out in 1943. The VPGS-41 (*Vintovka Protivotankovoye Granata Simonova*) rod-type antitank rifle grenade, which did not require a launcher, was merely inserted in the rifle; it was withdrawn in 1942. It had poor penetration and short range, and repeated firing damaged the rifle. Another infantry weapon that was quickly withdrawn was the 37mm "spade mortar." The hinged blade served as a base plate and a monopod was stowed in the barrel. It had only a 300-yard range, its tiny bomb was ineffective, and it made a poor shovel.

Use was made of captured German arms, especially after the USSR went on the offensive in 1943. Soldiers sought 9mm Luger P08 and Walther P38 pistols, 9mm MP40 machine pistols, 7.9mm MG34 and MG42 machine guns, hand grenades, hand mines, and the *Panzerfaust*, which they called a *Faust*. This antitank projector was especially valuable owing to the lack of comparable Soviet light, portable antitank weapons. Colored pyrotechnic flares were fired from a compact 26.5mm signal pistol, and this could fire captured German signal cartridges.

Scouts cautiously search a peasant's cabin. The Germans might leave a few rearguards behind to harass, but the real danger was booby traps. This PPS-40 submachine-gun-armed soldier has an RGD-33 blast grenade at the ready. (Nik Cornish Collection L50)

3. See Osprey Elite 124, *World War II Infantry Anti-Tank Tactics*, Osprey, Oxford (2005)
4. See Osprey New Vanguard 54, *Infantry Mortars of World War II*, Osprey, Oxford (2002)

Sappers search for mines using a mine probe and a VIM-210 mine detector fitted to a Mosin-Nagant rifle. A three-section aluminum pole was also provided. Sappers fought right alongside riflemen.

Soviet rifle regiment crew-served weapons

7.62mm Maxim PM-10 heavy machine gun

7.62mm Degtyarev DS-39 machine gun

7.62mm Goryunov SG-43 machine gun

12.7mm Degtyarev-Shpahina DShK-38 heavy machine gun

14.5mm Degtyarev PTRD-41 antitank rifle

14.5mm Simonov PTRS-41 antitank rifle

50mm RM-38, RM-39, RM-40, and RM-41 light mortars

82mm BM-36, BM-37, and BM-41 medium mortars

107mm PBHM-38 mountain heavy mortar

120mm HM-38 and HM-43 heavy mortars

37mm M1930 and M1932 antitank guns

45mm M1932, M1937, and M1942 antitank guns

76mm M1927/39 and M1943 regimental infantry guns

125mm ampoule antitank projector*

An ampulomet (antitank mortar) projecting an incendiary-agent filled glass sphere. It was ineffectively used from 1941 to 1942.

Personal equipment

The rifleman's equipment was simple and functional. At the beginning of the war the equipment was of generally good quality. Because of the massive losses, sudden shortage of materials, and the demands of mass production, simplified designs began to be fielded.

The 1936 equipment was of modern design and well made. The backpack was of the rucksack type with two small flap-closed pockets. The securing straps for the main compartment and the pouch flaps were made of leather. Straps were provided on the bottom to fasten a small pouch carrying pegs, pole sections, and guy rope to make the shelter-cape into a two-man tent when paired with another man's. The shoulder straps and back were padded. Inside the main compartment were carried a change of underwear, footwraps, rations, small cooking pot, and maybe a cup. The toilet kit and rifle cleaning kit were carried in the external pockets. The greatcoat and shelter-cape were carried in a horseshoe roll strapped to the pack. If the pack was not used the greatcoat and shelter-cape were carried as a bedroll over the left shoulder and the ends strapped or tied together at the right hip. Small essential items were carried in the roll. A 1.5in.-wide dark-brown leather belt was issued. On either side of the belt's front was a leather two-pocket rifle cartridge pouch, each pocket holding two five-round charger clips for a total of 40 rounds. A canvas reserve cartridge pouch was on the belt's back, holding six five-round clips. A cloth bandoleer might be issued for 14 more clips to carry a *boyekomplekt* (full complement) of ammunition. In place of the reserve cartridge pouch a

Riflemen were sometimes issued a 75x150cm camouflage net, which would be garnished with local vegetation to conceal themselves and their fighting positions.

ration bag was often carried. The entrenching tool and water bottle (which held just under 1 quart) were attached over the right hip. The cover was a simple bag, sometimes with a drawstring, with a buttoned cloth strap to secure the water bottle. The gas mask was carried on the left side suspended by a strap over the right shoulder. By 1942 gas masks were mostly turned in as unnecessary, but maintained in depots. *Bolshaya sapyornaya lopata* (entrenching tools) had either a pointed or square blade. The carrier was square-shaped with the flap secured by a leather strap and buckle or a cloth strap and button. Some men carried a small hatchet inside a canvas carrier.

Much of the early-issue equipment was lost during the defensive battles of 1941 and their mass loss of troops. Its production ceased and to replace it extremely simple and low-quality equipment was issued. Coarse canvas and thin webbing were used and shoddy leather or artificial substitutes were introduced, such as rubber-impregnated canvas. Fabric colors varied and were sometimes mixed in the same item. Most items were dark-tan or light olive-drab. The new belt was 1.5in. wide canvas reinforced by a 0.75in. leather strip. Fittings and fasteners were cheap metal, plastic buttons, wooden toggles and loops, or tie-tapes. Leather cartridge pouches were still issued, but also artificial leather and canvas. One- to three-pocket canvas hand grenade pouches were also issued along with special pouches for other weapons' magazines. Often soldiers were not issued complete sets of equipment, making do with what was available.

The 1941 *veshhevoi meshok* (simple backpack) was a canvas sack with a drawstring top closure, and was actually a revived World War I design. A U-shaped shoulder strap was attached to the bottom of the pack and the "top" of the "U" was simply knotted around the puckered top closure in such a manner as to adjust the strap's length to the wearer. A buckled chest strap held the shoulder straps in place. Basically the same items found in the 1936 pack were carried. The shelter-cape tent items, ration bag, and reserve cartridge pouch were seldom issued. Glass water bottles with cork stoppers were often substituted for metal.

The soldier to the right carries a simple backpack filled with his meager possessions and is armed with a German 9mm MP40 machine pistol, a prized find as it offered better penetration through typical cover than Soviet 7.62mm submachine guns.

Troops eat their meal from the standard mess kit, a simple pot, in a well-constructed trench. Porridge and soups were typical fare. (Nik Cornish Collection K58)

Often not even a pack was issued. Everything was carried in an over-the-shoulder bedroll of the greatcoat and shelter-cape which could also be carried with the simple backpack. There were instances where soldiers went into combat without a single item of equipment, carrying their ammunition in trouser pockets.

Personal items were spartan. A *perevgzochnii paket* (wound dressing packet) was carried in a tunic pocket; it was a light gray cloth with red markings. A soldier would be fortunate to have a small towel and toothbrush. Toothpaste and powder were almost unheard of luxuries, and often soap was just as rare. Usually a stick with a chewed end sufficed for a toothbrush, birch being particularly good for this. The soldier might have a comb, pocket mirror, and straight razor, often shared within his section. Someone in the section had a sewing kit, a little folding five-pocket canvas pouch with needles, thread, thimble, and buttons. Such items might be carried in a small cloth bags or simply rolled up in a towel. Cigarette lighters were made from 12.7mm cartridge cases by soldering on a flint igniter wheel. Commercial lighters were used but scarce, as were common wooden matches. Not every soldier was issued with weapons cleaning gear, but a few sets were carried by a section. A two-compartment tin container held oil and solvent. A tan cloth envelope-like pouch with tie tapes held a bore guide, dual-purpose tool (screwdriver, and firing pin protrusion gauge), cleaning rod handle, and cleaning jag.

The prewar mess kit was similar to the German version, but more commonly issued was a small cook pot with a pail handle. An enameled plate and cup were carried by most troops, along with a spoon. Recruits were directed to bring a spoon, which they tucked into a boot, when reporting for duty. A small utility or hunting knife was frequently carried, more as a tool than a weapon. Popular types were the *finka* and Finnish *puukko*; each had a short, broad blade with a leather sheath fully enclosing the knife up to its pommel.

Officers were issued a quality brown leather belt with an open-faced rectangular buckle and shoulder strap, haversack, leather-trimmed canvas map case, 6x30 B-1 binoculars, wrist compass, wristwatch, and a brown leather pistol or revolver holster.

C: Field feeding

C

D: Front fighting

E: Scouts manning an observation post

E

F

2a

2b

1

3

4

5

6

7

8

10a

10b

10c

9

G

1

2

3

CONDITIONS OF SERVICE

The degree of discipline, state of quarters, quality and abundance of food, sanitation conditions, standard of training, and the availability of equipment and training facilities varied greatly due to the size of the Red Army and the desperate wartime situation. A soldier from one unit might report that he received quality food during training while another said he nearly starved, receiving mostly spoiled food while the good food was sold on by the cooks.

Quarters could be any structure that would serve the purpose. One unit might be quartered in heated barracks with two-tier bunks, mattresses, and pillows. Often only two- and three-tier plank sleeping platforms were provided. The soldiers might be issued two sheets, a pillow case, and a brown cotton blanket. Mattresses and pillows were usually stuffed with straw by the soldiers themselves. Quarters were cramped, as the mass influx of troops did not allow the regulation 515 cubic feet per person (about 6x8ft to be floor space). Other troops slept outdoors on straw on the ground with a thin blanket. Tents were sometimes available, usually with straw on the floor, or even cots. Soldiers might also be quartered in village houses and barns, in which case they were often fed by civilians. Peasant log cabins – *izbushka, izba* for short – were often drafty and lice-infested. Families might be turned out or remain to feed the troops. In the rear areas troops might be quartered in public buildings, offices and business establishments, schools, warehouses, or any other available shelter.

Latrines with running water were inadequate or inoperable, making latrine pits necessary. Kitchen facilities were often poorly maintained and unsanitary. Garbage was infrequently disposed. In general, sanitation was poor, resulting in boils, diarrhea, stomach disorders, tuberculosis, and a variety of other disorders. Troops were to visit a *banya* every ten days and exchange underwear. In practice it might only be once or twice a month.

A captain of sappers is grateful for the delivery of a food parcel from home, regardless of its condition. He displays the old-style rank and branch insignia on a blue-piped black collar tab, which was replaced by shoulder straps in 1943. (Nik Cornish Collection A60)

Food

Red Army rations were frequently dismal. Food shortages were serious during the early defeats and retreats. The early loss of the Ukraine, the USSR's bread basket, caused serious shortages and worsened just a few months later with the onset of winter. Often villagers, voluntarily or under orders, provided food, which was known as "grandmother's rations" and typically consisted of boiled chickens and potatoes. But an army with thousands of troops could not live off the land, especially during mobile warfare. There were instances of only bread and butter for breakfast and for dinner a small wash tube of boiled beetroots was eaten communally. There was no lunch. Soldiers seldom had money to purchase food locally, which had been driven to exorbitantly high prices. Conditions did improve somewhat after 1943, but there were always shortages.

Regimental and divisional bakeries produced black bread, a main staple, here to be delivered to frontline units by a *pulk* sled drawn by a sturdy Bashkir pony. (Nik Cornish Collection A47)

Armies and fronts possessed rear service organizations, which foraged and purchased food, harvested crops, and raised livestock. Butter, grains, and vegetables were purchased locally by the army rations and fodder division. Divisions possessed flour mills to grind grain, and livestock were delivered on the hoof to regimental kitchens. Captured German food stocks were valued. As in all armies, the rear service troops were unpopular and were referred to as *krysa* (rats) or *tylovaya krysa* (rear rats) by the frontline riflemen.

Much of the field ration was bread, canned meats, and fresh and preserved vegetables. Dried peas were issued in packaged blocks. Black rye bread was baked in regimental bakeries. Tinned meats included *tushonka* (stewed pork or beef – very greasy) and tinned herring and other fish such as *kilka* and *bichki* (cooked in tomato sauce when available). Spam (canned lunch meat) was provided through Lend-Lease by the United States and called *vtoroy front myaso* (second front meat). Stalin credited it with saving the Red Army. Another Lend-Lease food was *Rosevelt yaitsa* (Roosevelt eggs) – powdered eggs. Salted herring and *moskovskaya* (summer sausage) supplemented meat rations. Grits, macaroni, and vermicelli (thin spaghetti) were issued along with cooking oil and *salo* (pork back fat).

Two of the most common dishes were *shchi* and *kasha*, resulting in a soldier's slogan – *Shchi ee kasha, pisha nasha* (*Shchi* and *kasha*, that's our fare). The Russian soldier was already familiar with them. *Shchi* is cabbage soup made with meat broth, although water frequently replaced the broth. Potatoes, carrots, and onions might be added, though seldom did they grace the dish on the frontline. The Russian spelling is ЩИ, which transliterates as *shchi* in English and in German as *Schtschi*, leading to the Russians saying the Fritz made eight errors spelling a two-letter word. *Kasha* was a roasted buckwheat groats porridge boiled in water and salt. *Kasha*

Unit officers share vodka and black bread after a briefing, a common practice. The officer to the left wears the *shuba* sheepskin coat. All wear the popular *shapka-ushanka*). (Nik Cornish Collection L55)

might be considered a breakfast food, but like *shchi*, might have been served as any meal's main course. *Kasha* made with millet was known as "shrapnel" owing to hard uncooked grains. Boiled potatoes and potato soup (*kartofel' sup*) were also served along with *borsch* (beet soup with carrots and onions). A rare treat was *kissel*, stewed fruit thickened with cornstarch.

The standard beverage was *chai* (hot sugared tea), often brewed in a liberated charcoal-fired *samovar*. Real Russian tea is brewed in a small amount of water to make a concentrate. This is poured into a glass to which boiling water and sugar are added. Beer, cognac, and vodka were also issued. The *Narkom 100-gramm* (People's Commissariat of Defense 100-gram [3.5oz]) described the supposed daily issue of vodka. Soldiers had a reputation for drinking anything. Vodka was a drug of sorts and there is truth to the stories of units being deliberately intoxicated before driven to attack.

The Soviet soldier's ration included tobacco and cigarette papers. *Makhorka* was a poor, cheap, finely chopped tobacco. Soldiers rolled their own cigarettes using *makhorka* and whatever paper they could find, usually newspaper. Before the war no Western-style cigarettes were produced. There were only *papierossi*, paper tubes with the front one-third filled with tobacco. Officers were issued better commercial cigarettes such as the Kazbek brand. Field exchanges were available down to division-level where soldiers could buy toiletry items, paper and pencils, etc. There were also canteens serving tea and snacks, and barber shops.

Meals were prepared by company or battalion field kitchens such as the PK-43 mobile kitchen. If at all possible a hot breakfast and dinner were served. Hard biscuits, sausage or bacon or canned meat, and tea would be provided for lunch and on operations that took the soldiers away from the kitchens. Alternatively, if supplies were short they might receive only a *soldat buterbrod* (soldiers' sandwich), a single slice of black bread.

Medical care

Medical care was marginal. Each higher echelon was responsible for evacuating casualties from their subordinate units; for example, the battalion sent two litter teams to each company. Ideally, two doctors operated the battalion aid station. Individuals in platoons were trained as medics as a secondary duty. Dressings, instruments, and procedures were usually inadequate and outdated. Sulfa drugs and other antibiotics were scarce and morphine almost unheard of. Illness was a major problem and most Russians had not received preventive inoculations as in Western countries. Peasant remedies were often the soldiers' only resort. Particular problems were encountered with typhus, pneumonia, dysentery, meningitis, tuberculosis, diphtheria, and malaria. Frostbite and trench foot caused massive casualties. Lice were also a serious problem. Periodic lice checks were to be made, called a "Form 20." The visits to *banya* served to rid the troops of lice and their uniforms were supposed to be laundered and steamed, but this was impossible during prolonged field duty. Troops spent a lot of time picking lice out from uniforms. One method of lice removal was to bury the uniform with a collar tip poking out of the cold ground and burn emerging lice with a cigarette.

A cook mixes a concoction, probably for the unit's officers, as enlisted men's food was prepared in large batches while officers received special rations. (Nik Cornish A22)

A recalled reservist lights up a *makhorka* cigarette. They were traditionally rolled in a "fat" manner in whatever paper was available. Some soldiers developed a fondness for them and continued to smoke them after the war. (Nik Cornish Collection K55)

A *sanitar* (medic) treats a wounded soldier beside a Maxim 7.62mm PM-10 heavy machine gun, a valuable support weapon. Hasty fighting positions have been scraped in the ground, but their parapets would not stop a rifle bullet except at extreme range.

Soyuz denii – Soviet money

The basic Soviet monetary unit was the *rubl'* (ruble), which was divided into 100 *kopeika* (kopecks or kop.). However, an additional currency unit supplemented the ruble from 1922–47, the *chervonets* (ten), worth 10 rubles. There was no official symbol for a ruble, although a Cyrillic "P" (Latin "R") was often used. The "official" exchange rate was US$1 to 5R, 30 kopecks, a rate maintained from 1937–50, while a pound sterling was 21R, 20 kopecks. The conversion rate is purely subjective, and a much lesser rate was actually used since legal trade between the USSR and the West was restricted. Coinage was issued in 1, 2, 3, 5, 10, 15, 20, and 50 kopecks; rubles in 1, 3 and 5R notes; and *chervonets* for denominations of 10R (1 *chervonets*) and higher – 3, 5, and 10 *chervonets* notes.

Pay

Soldiers were paid once a month, but often they never saw the money unless in the rear. All or part of the pay could be allotted to next-of-kin, but this was sometimes impossible owing to massive civilian displacements and casualties. Often pay was held and at some future time the soldier would receive back pay. Soldiers were, however, exempt from taxes. The 1943 base pay was 600R (rubles) for a private, 1,000R for a corporal, 2,000R for a junior sergeant, and 3,000R for a sergeant. There were categories of special pay, including field pay to combat troops, Guards units, antitank, and tank troops (50 percent base pay), jump pay for paratroopers (25R per jump), and bonuses for the award of certain decorations. Allotments were also paid to fathers over 60; mothers over 55; invalided parents, wives, and children; and children under 16.

Punishment

The Red Army legal system was complex, with no single regulation codifying all crimes and misdemeanors and under the control of no single agency. The type of punishment, its extent, and on what rank categories it could be imposed depended on the command echelon. For example, a section commander or assistant platoon commander could warn, privately reprimand, reprimand in ranks, delay discharge by one week, or assign one day's extra fatigue to his men. A company commander could reprimand all subordinates, reprimand soldiers in ranks, delay discharge six weeks for soldiers and four for sergeants, assign extra fatigues to soldiers for eight days and sergeants for four, arrest soldiers for ten days and sergeants for five, hold a Comrade's Court of soldiers and sergeants, forbid leave, or confine to quarters for three days.

By regulation the only crimes for which the death penalty and confiscation of property were allowed were desertion by both enlisted men and officers and absence without leave by officers. In reality, officers and enlisted were also executed for cowardliness, retreating or ordering retreat without authority, aiding the enemy, and spying.

The disciplinary system included encouragements and awards bestowed on men who conducted themselves conscientiously and assiduously in their duties. They might have been given expressions of gratitude in the ranks or in orders of the day, granted extra off-duty time,

Mail call at the company command post. Most Soviet photographs were posed and censored, resulting in a less than accurate portrayal of the soldier's life.

have been presented with valuable gifts or monetary awards, or have any disciplinary penalties withdrawn. Units also received decorations and honorific titles for battles as a means of improving morale.

Entertainment

The importance of entertainment was recognized as a means of improving troop morale and a further method for disseminating propaganda and improving motivation. Coordinated by political officers known as *politruk* (see below), motion pictures were shown on outdoor screens. These were not purely propaganda movies; even selected American films were shown. Military-organized musical, dance, and singing troupes also conducted tours, all emphasizing Russian culture and traditions. The *balalaika*, a small string instrument, was revived as the Russian national instrument, with the government encouraging its use and forming *balalaika* orchestras.

Sex was an issue handled almost prudishly by the Soviet government. Basically, it did not exist. The official policy was that the focus of men was to fight the war and work the factories or fields, while women maintained the home and raised children, whose source was never explained. The reality was that women worked in industry and agriculture and even the armed forces alongside men. With the civilian population mobilized there was no idyllic home awaiting soldiers such as was touted in propaganda.

The Red Army did not provide field brothels. In the rear areas unofficial brothels emerged, but they were not widespread. As far as can be determined the Red Army was the only World War II army that did not issue condoms, resulting in increased venereal disease, for which there were severe penalties. Rapes occurred on an epidemic scale once the Red Army entered Germany. However, this had little to do with sex; it was the basest form of revenge and humiliation the soldiers could inflict on the Germans. There were instances where rapists were executed, but these were exceptions to the norm, which was to condone and even encourage such practices.

Local civilians, joined by a soldier, perform a traditional dance for soldiers. Army dance and music troupes performed for soldiers and gave a great morale boost. (Nik Cornish Collection BA179)

It was common for commanders and occasionally soldiers to "adopt" *pokhodno-polevy zheny* (field marching wives) or PPZh – a play on the designation for the PPSh-41 submachine gun. Officers would sometimes enter these camp followers on unit rosters and assign them duty positions for rationing purposes. A chauvinistic attitude existed toward female soldiers, with all suspected of having sold or traded themselves for sexual favors. After the war, it was said of women wearing decorations *za boevye zaslugi* ("for military service") that the decorations actually meant *za polevya zaslugi* ("for sexual service").

ON CAMPAIGN

It is often said the Soviet soldier was immune to discomfort, pain, and cold. He could endure endless suffering and hunger owing to his previous harsh civilian life. He could march endlessly without sleep and food and would keep going under the most hopeless and brutal conditions. Russians, however, are humans like anyone else. They kept going because they had no choice.

A Guards private carries two German weapons, a Panzerfaust 60 and an Eihgr.38 "egg grenade." The Panzerfaust was considered a valuable capture and widely used because the Red Army fielded no comparable light, portable, one-man antitank weapon. The soldier wears the Guards badge on his right breast and the Order of Glory on his left. The orange-and-black striped decoration was the most common valor award. The Medal for Victory over Germany used the same ribbon, but with a round medal. (Nik Cornish Collection BA142)

Army commanders and military councils were directed by Stalin to:

a) In all circumstances remove from office commanders and commissars who allowed their troops to retreat without authorization by the army command and send them to the Military Councils of the Fronts for court-martial;

b) Form 3–5 well-armed *zagradotryads* [guards (barrage) units], deploy them in the rear of unstable divisions, and oblige them to execute panic-mongers and cowards on site in case of panic and chaotic retreat, thus giving faithful soldiers a chance to do their duty before the Motherland;

c) Form 5–10 penal companies where soldiers and sergeants who have broken discipline due to cowardice or instability should be sent. These units should be deployed in the most difficult sectors, thus giving these soldiers an opportunity to redeem their crimes against the Motherland by blood. [They performed mine clearance, sometimes by simply being herded through the minefield, and other tasks included obstacle emplacement or breaching under fire, recovering bodies, etc.]

No officer had the authority to call for the withdrawal of his unit. That could only come from higher headquarters. The barrage units, formed of reliable combat veterans, did not hesitate to shoot down retreating soldiers. They themselves were exempt from direct combat, unless they faltered.

Bivouac

Soviet fighting positions were just that and no consideration was given to living in them. Small circular or rectangular one-man foxholes were the usual rifleman's position. The Germans called this a "Russian hole." Soldiers often dug shallow, full-body-length slit trenches for protection from shelling and bombing. Slit trenches were often dug as sleeping shelters.

Guards
The first *Gvardiya* (Guards) formations were designated on September 18, 1941, by Order No.308 of the People's Commissar of Defense for distinguished service during the August 30–September 8 Yelnva Offensive. The 100th, 127th, 153rd, and 161st Rifle divisions were redesignated the 1st, 2nd, 3rd, and 4th Guards Rifle Divisions, respectively. The divisions' organic units also received the Guards title. Many other units would be so honored. Guards units received the Guards Red Banner and from May 21, 1942, "Guards" preceded rank titles and the Guards Badge was authorized for wear on the right breast. Guards rankers were entitled to double pay, commanders and sergeants to one-and-a-half pay, and the units were authorized increased allocations of crew-served weapons, additional manning, and better rations. The Guards Badge had a gold wreath, white enamel center with a red enamel star, and red enamel banner with Cyrillic "Guards" in gold. (Badge courtesy of Tony Miller, 147th Guards Rifle Regiment – reenactment)

In the defense a rifle platoon dug one-man fighting holes, but if the position was occupied long enough these were connected by trenches. Here troops move down the trench to reinforce another sector. They wear the old Kaska-36 helmet. (Nik Cornish Collection L48)

A shell-blasted Maxim machine-gun position. The rifleman still holds a five-round charger clip in his left hand. Such small round one-man fighting positions were called *russischloch* or *rusloch* (Russian holes) by the Germans.

Sleeping in the open was a frequent requirement. There are numerous accounts of soldiers sleeping in their greatcoats; no blankets or sleeping bags were issued. There was more to it than just bundling up in a coat, however. Soldiers slept in pairs. A bed of pine or fir boughs, piled leaves or evergreen needles, straw, or cut grass was laid and covered with a shelter-cape. (The soldiers might dig a pit in the snow or a double-wide slit trench as the bed's foundation.) The bed was essential for protection from wet or cold ground, mud, or snow. Two soldiers lay down on their sides, spooned front-to-back with knees curled. They placed one greatcoat over their legs with its shoulders over their feet and the hem came up to their shoulders. Their booted feet were tucked up in the coat's shoulders. The second coat was placed with its shoulders over their heads, which were protected by caps and wrapped scarves. Its hem reached down past their knees. They sometimes had the luxury of wrapping up in a liberated blanket or two. This whole arrangement would be covered by the second shelter-cape. Warm on one side and cold on the other, they would periodically turn to their other side in unison. Such accommodations, however, were inadequate for below-freezing conditions.

Fighting against the elements

The weather conditions were brutal or at least difficult throughout the USSR. The Russian winter, *Generál Moróz* (General Frost), was an enemy to both sides and certainly in some areas the Red Army was no more prepared than the Germans. In the north the first snows appeared in mid-September and about five weeks later in the south. Temperatures plunged to -20°F and even as low as -60°F. Vehicles could not move in the snow, draught horses, on which artillery and supply columns relied, died en masse, troops suffered every form of extreme cold-weather injury and illness, weapons failed to function, shells and grenades were smothered in the snow, and land mines froze solid. Spring emerged in April and May and with it came massive snowmelt and rains. Sucking, sticky mud pulled off high-topped boots and added so much weight to the feet that it became painful and difficult to walk. If laboriously scraped off it would

build back in a dozen steps. Trucks and even tanks became mired. More tanks were bogged down in the mud and abandoned than were lost to enemy fire. The short summer was hot, dry, and dusty. With the equally short autumn came massive, flooding rains and the *rasputitsa* (big mud), which was even worse than the spring mud.

BELIEF AND BELONGING

The USSR comprised over 100 ethnic groups, including south-central Asians, Finnic peoples in the north, Turkic groups in the Urals, Caucasians in the Caucasus Mountains, and Far Eastern Asiatic groups. Some 85 percent of the Soviet population was Slav (Russians, Ukrainians, Byelorussians). In total, the Soviet Union encompassed 150 languages and dialects. Russian, however, was the language of command within the Red Army.

Citizens of the USSR were identified on their personal documents as either *Russky*, a Russian-speaking Slav from "Great Russia," or *Rossiyanin*, meaning a "citizen of Russia." Their papers were marked with their *natsional'nost*, which did not mean country of origin, but ethnic background. *Natsmen* was a collective derogatory term for minorities.

With a few notable exceptions, the Soviets did not form national or ethnic units. It was preferred to mix ethnic groups throughout units in small numbers rather than risk mutinies, nationalistic problems, and the propagation of counter-revolutionary ideas by banding them together. The majority of the Red Army was composed of Slavs – there was simply too much distrust of other ethnic groups. It was even preferred to mix Slavs from different regions among units, as the Soviets strove to blur any form of national and regional identity, preferring for soldiers and citizens to identify with the USSR and communism first. By *sliianie* (blending) all nationalities would be merged into one, eliminating ethnic identity and national consciousness.

The most notable of the ethnic units were the Cossacks. A quasi-ethnic group, Cossacks are a mix of Russian, Ukrainian, and even have

Greek and Turkish blood. Groups lived all over southern Russia in their own communities with their own culture. They were also a political organization, believing in independence from a national government. National units were raised in the former Baltic States, Lithuania, Latvia, and Estonia, being organized from existing units and because they spoke their own languages.

With its men officially united under communism, the reality for the Red Army was that being composed of so many diverse ethnic groups, combined with a natural distrust of strangers, meant there was little true unity on a large scale prior to the war. The Red Army served as a melting pot and only the hatred of the German invaders served to unify the masses, at least in the desire to destroy a common enemy. Rifle units did achieve cohesion, though, as did any military organization, through the shared experience of combat. Unending propaganda and political indoctrination efforts reinforced this. Once in combat no one cared about their comrades' nationality. "We were all bleeding the same blood," said one *frontovik.*

Officially atheistic, the Communist Party essentially replaced organized religion and Lenin was its "god." All government and Party officials professed atheism and practiced official repression of religion. Nevertheless, many Russians remained somewhat faithful to the Russian Orthodox Church. Although Stalin relaxed wartime restrictions on attending church, there were still no chaplains. Millions in the newly occupied Baltic States and other western areas were Roman Catholics. In the south-central republics were huge numbers of practicing Muslims. There were also large numbers of Jews. Russia was known for its anti-Semitism, but Jewish soldiers often reported that they experienced little of this in fighting units.

Political indoctrination, called "political work," was a key part of military life, consisting of lectures on the communist system, current events, and motivational and morale-building activities. Usually one hour

A platoon commander reads excerpts from a newspaper to his SVT-40 rifle-armed men. Such readings were a standard means of keeping troops informed, building morale, and reinforcing belief and belonging. Many soldiers were illiterate or could not read very well. (Nik Cornish Collection T50)

a day was dedicated to political work. News and current events, according to the Party, were usually read directly from state or army newspapers. Soviet victories were of course touted and defeats underplayed or not mentioned. Nor was the participation of the Western Allies addressed. The exploits of decorated individual soldiers and units were read to inspire the troops. It was made perfectly clear to the troops that the USSR was fighting for national survival against a merciless enemy – *Smert Fascistam Sebakim!* (Death to the Fascist Dogs!) was the rallying cry.

The Soviets were taught to hate the Germans, hence Soviet terms for them were less than complimentary. The official term was *fashist* (fascist, plural *fashistskii*). Soviets never used Nazi as it included the word "socialist" – National-Sozialistische Deutsche Arbeiterpartei (National Socialist German Workers' Party) and the Soviets considered their government to be "socialist" in philosophy. *Gitlerit* (Hitlerite – there is no "H" in Russian) was another common term, as was *Germanskii* (Russianized German). *Nemets* (plural *Nemtsi*) was formal Russian for German; another term was *nyemetzi*, literally meaning dumb (as in mute).

The Pliticheskoe Upravlenie Krasnoi, Armii (Main Political Administration of the Commissariat of Defense; PURKKA) was responsible for supervising the Communist Party and Komsomol members in the Red Army, reinforcing the morale and political indoctrination of Red Army troops, political surveillance of commanders and staffs, and propaganda directed against the enemy.

Political officers known as *komissar* (commissars) were assigned to all echelons of command down to and including battalion level. They were assisted by small staffs to perform the above functions. They had more sinister powers as well – maintaining political surveillance of all commanders and soldiers through informers and unit leaders. Known as *seksot* (from *sekretnyj sotrudnik* – secret collaborator), informers were cultivated within units to report any defeatist, treacherous, and cowardly attitudes demonstrated by their comrades. They represented the "dual-

It was recognized that soldiers must be commended for their services. Here a commander congratulates a soldier before the ranks for successfully accomplishing his tasks.

command" concept; they had the power to countermand the orders and decisions of their unit commander. They also had the authority to assume command if a commander ordered a withdrawal. Few commissars had any military experience and relentlessly held to Stalin's directives of no retreat – "Not a step back!" There are countless examples of their interfering to cause more problems than they solved.

In October 1942 the commissars lost this authority and became "deputy commanders for political affairs" – *politruk*. They now focused on political work, but still maintained surveillance on troops and were responsible for punishments up to and including summary executions, called a *devyat gram* (nine grams, the weight of bullet), *pustit v raskhod* (to expend someone), or *vyshka* (from *vysshaya mera nakazanija* – extreme penalty). As there were no chaplains, the *politruk* fulfilled the role of morale-building and troop welfare. (They had to have been Communist Party members for at least three years.) The *politruk* evaluated training, rating the qualifications of individuals, submitted monthly reports on unit discipline, and organized lectures, discussions, Party festivities, and entertainment. If overdoing it, holding too strongly to the Party line, or interfering too much with the unit, the *politruk* might find themselves being ignored by the troops and even have their activities curtailed by the commander.

There were no *politruk* at company level, but the commander was assigned these responsibilities even if he was not a Party member. Additionally, units had an Vsesoyuzny Leninskiy Kommunisticheskiy Soyuz Molodyozhi (All-Union Leninist Young Communist League; VLKSM), also known as Komsomol. Komsomol representatives – *komsorg* – in

A conference of the officers of a rifle regiment. The officer standing next to the regimental commander, with a satchel slung over his back, is probably the deputy commander for political affairs – *politruk*. The *politruk* wore no insignia to identify him as such. (Nik Cornish Collection L57)

companies could be of any rank. The company Komsomol organizer was usually a senior sergeant. The Komsomol was very active in some units, holding rallies and even openly criticizing commanders. Many young soldiers, especially from the cities, had been members of the Vsesoyuznaya Pionerskaya Organizatsiya Imeni V.I. Lenina (All-Union Pioneer Organization in the Name of V.I. Lenin) or "Young Pioneers" from age 10–15, at which age they could join the Komsomol on their road to Party membership.

Not just anyone could join the Party to become a true *tovarschch* (comrade) – non-Party members were addressed as *tovarschchi*, a mocking term used by the White Russians during the Civil War. Candidates had to demonstrate reliability and a true dedication to communist ideology. Three Party-member sponsors, who had known them for at least a year, needed to vouch for candidates. Once accepted they were on one-year probation. At the end of 1941, candidates who had distinguished themselves in combat only had to be known to their sponsors for a short time and the probationary period was reduced to three months. One of the reported benefits of Party membership was that if a non-Party soldier was killed in combat it was not always reported to his next-of-kin, while Party member deaths were. This may not have been completely true, especially after the Red Army's administration improved in late 1943 and after the massive early-war losses. Komsomol and Party membership increased later in the war owing not only to its benefits, but to growing patriotism, which came from success and increasing sacrifices.

The soldiers' view of their immediate commanders was generally favorable. As in any army, the troops were suspicious of higher headquarters. Unit commanders frequently developed good relations with their men, and were treated as a *soratnik* (comrade in arms), sharing the same dangers and privations. Commanders were secondary school graduates with the same or slightly higher education level than their men. Few were university graduates, but there was no real class distinction as there was no true middle or "elite" class. Troops typically called their company commander their *Batya* (Father). In the "classless society" commanders did receive benefits, however, including better rations than their men, although in the front line they usually ate what their men did.

EXPERIENCE IN BATTLE

The following actions are fictitious, but are a combination of incidents from actual events. The dates and locations are immaterial in regards to understanding the experiences of the *frontoviki*.

They had marched all night trudging down frozen roads, pushing through knee-deep snow over fields and through fir forests. They had last eaten breakfast the morning before – there had been no food or rest since. The troops were utterly exhausted and cold to the bone. Now they moved in starts and stops deep into the forest. Artillery could be heard in the near distance, but no flashes seen. The riflemen were finally ordered to move up a side trail to an area of milling men and stacked boxes. Filing through the trees they were given clips of rifle cartridges, four hand grenades, packets of *makhorka*, and the machine gunners filled up every pocket with handfuls of loose cartridges for their pan

magazines. At the end of the line their cups were filled with hot sweet tea, the mess pot was filled to the brim with *shchi*, and a chunk of bread was handed to them. Moving farther up the trail they wolfed down the food before it froze. Orders came to move farther into the woods. They cut fir boughs to sit on, huddled together for warmth. No fires were allowed as this would have given away their position to the enemy. After too short a time they were roused out of their off-and-on slumber and issued their *Narkom 100-gramm* of vodka, something they had not seen in days.

They were on the move again with orders to remain absolutely silent, breaking up into subunits and dispersing into the woods. The platoon was led to a point and placed on line. Other platoons were positioned on their flanks. As the sun rose behind them they could make out that they were some 100 yards inside a forest. Without warning, Russian black shell bursts rippled across the close horizon.

The barrage continued as the platoons were aligned and readied. There were shouts and red flares, and the riflemen began moving forward with supporting Maxims rattling off long bursts. The artillery lifted, but they still had 400 yards of thigh-deep snow to cross. There was a sound like ripping paper and streams of red and white tracers swept over the snow, accompanied by the muffled thumps of their mortars being fired. Churning through the thigh-deep snow, their advance was painfully slow. Men fell in droves to shrapnel and bullets and the platoon commander beat his troops forward with his entrenching tool. The German defenses consisted of a barbed-wire barrier, half buried in snow, and men tangled in the wire were easy targets for the German defenders. A hoarse "*Urra*" was heard and men took up the guttural shout. Grenades were thrown, and the riflemen leapt into the snow trenches, but the surviving Germans had fled to a safer position in the rear.

The soldiers searched the dugouts and sergeants shouted and shoved men into position, trying to reorganize them for the inevitable counterattack. German mortar rounds were already beginning to fall, soon followed by artillery shells. All the riflemen could do was huddle

in the trenches and endure the seemingly endless concussions and whining fragments. The barrage covered the first rifle cracks of the "Hitlerite" counterattack. There was little to it and the Germans quickly fell back, having made little effort to reclaim their positions. It had been a feint attack to delay any further advance as the Hitlerites laid mines and strung more wire. Out of the platoon of 36, the riflemen now numbered 22. The artillery barrage resumed and they knew they would soon assault the main German strongpoint.

* * *

As night fell, four *razvedchiki* (scouts) of a regimental reconnaissance platoon slipped through the brush, staying in the shadows cast by the faint moonlight filtering through the trees. They moved a short distance, stopping to lie on the ground and listen. In forest fighting it was impossible to know exactly where the enemy positions were. The only way was to wait patiently for the Germans to make a mistake – to light a cigarette, cough, or rattle one of the hand-warming tins they filled with hot pebbles from their bunker stoves. Their wait was rewarded with the faint flash of light as a bunker door's blackout curtain was quickly opened and closed over to their left. They heard whispers as one guard relieved another. Each bunker had a sentry, and they knew there would be another bunker to their right. The dark shape of the relieved sentry skulked to the rear. The patrol commander moved forward as quickly as caution permitted. They were behind the bunkers now, lying in a low clump of bushes behind a muddy trail. From within could be heard groans; diarrhea was a common infection among the troops. One German finally emerged and, as he passed, the two largest Scouts leapt on him, slamming their fists into his body. With a *finka* held against his throat he submitted. They waited to see if an alarm had been raised. Satisfied the scuttle had not been heard, the Scouts crept back with their gagged prisoner.

Troops rush into the assault. There was little in the way of fire and maneuver, just a mass advance reminiscent of World War I.

A DP machine-gun crew covers the advance of their section. The assistant gunner might be armed with a rifle, carbine, or submachine gun.

Just forward of the bunkers, without warning, a rifle cracked. Two of the Russian patrol immediately each threw two grenades at the bunker, then covered their faces to prevent the flash from the detonations from temporarily blinding them. As German machine guns opened fire, they rushed back to the Russian positions. The prisoner would be taken to the command post. Called a *yaziki* (tongue) he would be forced to talk.

* * *

Far from the frozen fields, small battles raged in the streets of the towns and cities of Mother Russia. In one such town Russian riflemen urgently strengthened their positions in anticipation of a German attack, including the fortification of a liberated house. Within the house some riflemen began hacking a loophole with bayoneted rifles about 1.5ft above the floor. Others were dragging away the bodies of the German defenders and those riflemen who had been killed in the earlier seizure of the property. The bodies of the Germans were looted for their water bottles, iron rations, and heating tablets. The furniture of the house was thrown down the stairs so that the entrance could be blocked. A washtub of sand was lugged in and set in a corner to douse fires. The section commander went to the window and scanned the street and buildings opposite. Closing the riddled shutters, he stood a bed stand against the window; its wire mesh would keep out grenades.

With the loophole finished the gunner set his Degtyarev down, lying behind it, and sighted through the hole. Two men pulled a heavy table from another room and positioned it over the Degtyarev for extra protection from falling debris. The observer fashioned an opening in the broken window shutter to drop grenades on anyone sheltering against the outside wall. They built a barricade in the far corner on the same wall in which the hall door was set. They turned a table on its side, stacked bed mattresses against it, and further protected the side toward the door with a cabinet. They could shelter behind this if a grenade was thrown in, and anyone entering would be shot from behind the corner-barricade. A short timber was found in the hall where the assault gun shell had blown a hole and the door was jammed shut with it.

As they waited for the assault, one man had written *Pobyeda!* (Victory!) in charcoal on the wall...

Across the Soviet Union, and eventually throughout Germany, small-scale actions such as this were repeated countless times. Although great battles at places such as Stalingrad, Kursk, and Kharkov were critical junctures in the struggle for the Eastern Front, the Soviet rifleman fought a constant war at a local level, each man contributing to the final German defeat.

THE AFTERMATH OF BATTLE

Germany surrendered on May 8, 1945 (V-E Day), but the surrender was ratified on the 9th, which the USSR recognizes as Victory Day. Victory was complete, but costly beyond imagination. Casualty estimates vary greatly depending on who did the counting, when they did it, and what territories they included. Out of a 1939 population of 1.685 million some 11.5 million civilians died along with approximately 1 million Holocaust victims. Official military deaths include 6.33 million killed in action, 550,000 missing, 556,000 non-combat deaths, 1.283 million prisoners dead out of 4.059 million taken captive, and millions wounded. (Western historians estimate that 3 million prisoners died out of 5.7 million.) Additionally, up to 1.5 million reservists are estimated to have died in 1941/42 before they were assigned to the active strength, plus 150,000 militia and 250,000 partisans. Total military and civilian loss estimates range from 20 to 27 million.

A DP light machine-gun crew takes cover beside a destroyed T-20 Komsomolets light artillery tractor (the opening is for a DT machine gun). The gunner carried only one 47-round pan magazine and the assistant three magazines in a special can.

Snowsuit-clad troops pass through a burned village. Both sides habitually burned buildings when retreating to deny the other side their shelter from the cold. Note that bayonets are not carried fixed, as was normal practice. (Nik Cornish Collection L31)

The flag of the Soviet Union is raised over a defeated Berlin – Victory Day.

Surviving veterans were honored and held in high esteem, bedecked with rows of medals and allowed to participate in annual parades. Countless monuments were erected throughout the USSR and liberated Eastern Europe. The disabled were cared for to the modest extent the USSR could provide. Servicemen and women received pensions based on time in service, wounds, and their decorations.

There was a bewildering array of decorations for valor, service, and campaign participation. Certain valor decorations were restricted to different rank categories. When granting additional decorations of the same order or class there was no means of indicating additional awards on the decoration. One simply wore additional decorations, resulting in the appearance of a great many decorations on some personnel. The decorations themselves were the property of the state and were to be turned in upon the holder's death and not kept by the family, and payment ceased when he died. For the Order of Lenin this was 25R, Order of the Red Banner 20R, and for the Order of the Red Star 15R. Award holders were also entitled to free tickets to cultural events (theater, opera, concerts), free local bus and trolley tickets, and a once-a-year free round-trip train ticket. Wounds received in combat, and even debilitating illnesses, were denoted by wound stripes worn over the right breast – red for minor wounds/illness and gold-yellow for serious. If a soldier was killed or missing in action, his parents or dependants, if they made less than 400R a month, would receive an extra 25 percent of their monthly wage for one soldier killed/missing, 45 percent for two, and 60 percent for three.

By war's end the Soviet armed forces numbered 11.365 million troops. Demobilization, however, started toward the end of 1945, and in a few years the armed forces fell to fewer than 3 million troops. Of all the Soviet forces fighting on the Eastern Front, the contribution of the riflemen was crucial. They were at the "sharp end" of the great Motherland's defense, fighting from the vast plains and forests to the streets of Soviet villages and towns, till they were at last victorious.

COLLECTIONS, MUSEUMS, AND REENACTMENT

Western collectors have found that authentic Soviet Great Patriotic War uniforms, insignia, and equipment are extremely rare and costly. There are few items on the market and few authoritative books covering the subject. Surprisingly, the most popular and obtainable collectors' pieces in America are Soviet small arms.

Museum collections of Soviet relics in the United States and Europe are generally small. The Western Allies had little contact with the Red Army and as it was an ally there was little motive to create museum displays. Little in the way of Red Army items have found their way to Western museums.

There are, however, scores of military museums in Russia and the various republics of the former USSR, ranging from national institutions to small local museums displaying relics collected in the area. There are a number of groups of amateur military archeologists who search for relics and remains on battlefields. They have even recovered tanks from lakes. Rather than personally keeping or selling the relics, they donate to local museums.

The premier museum is the Central Armed Forces Museum in Moscow. Other major museums include the Soviet Army Museum in Moscow; Military Historical Museum of Artillery, Engineers, and Signals in St Petersburg (formerly Leningrad); and the Tank Museum in Kubinka.

There are actually quite a number of Great Patriotic War reenactment groups in the United States, Britain, and Australia and of course a large number of German reenactors to challenge them. These groups emphasize their non-political/ideological portrayal of Red Army living history. The full range of replica period Soviet uniforms and equipment is available to reenactors.

A returning *frontovik* surveys the destruction inflicted by the Germans. He carries a simple backpack and a German mess tin.

Sergeants receive decorations. Their shoulder strap rank stripes and edge piping are in the rifle troops' raspberry red. Medals and orders suspended from ribbons were generally worn on the left breast and badges on the right, but there were exceptions. (Nik Cornish Collection K125)

A rifle company marches through a liberated German city. Loot is evident, and includes a guitar. This platoon's three sections appear to comprise six or seven men each. The assistant platoon commander brings up the rear. (Nik Cornish Collection AO96)

BIBLIOGRAPHY

Abdulin, Mansur, *Red Road from Stalingrad: Recollections of a Soviet Infantryman*, Pen and Sword, Barnsley, UK (2005)

Baker, A. J. and John Walter, *Russian Infantry Weapons of World War 2*, Arco Publishing, New York (1971)

Bessonov, Evgeni, *Tank Rider: Into the Reich with the Red Army*, Stackpole Books, Mechanicsburg, PA (2003)

Glantz, David (ed.), *Slaughterhouse: The Handbook of the Eastern Front*, Aberjona Press, Bedford, PA (2005)

Grossman, Vasily, *A Writer at War: Vasily Grossman with the Red Army, 1941–1945*, Pantheon Books, New York (2006)

Loza, Dmitriy F., *Commanding the Red Army's Sherman Tanks: The World War II Memoirs of Hero of the Soviet Union Dmitriy Loza*, University of Nebraska Press, Lincoln, NE (1997)

– *Fighting for the Soviet Motherland: Recollections from the Eastern Front*, University of Nebraska Press, Lincoln, NE (1998)

Lucas, James, *War on the Eastern Front: 1941–1945*, Stein and Day, New York (1979)

Merridale, Catherine, *Ivan's War: Life and Death in the Red Army, 1939–1945*, Metropolitan Books, New York (2006)

Shalito, Anton, *Red Army Uniforms of World War II in Colour Photographs*, Motorbooks International, Osceola, WI (1993)

Sharp, Charles S., *Soviet Infantry Tactics in World War II: Red Army Infantry Tactics from Squad to Rifle Company from the Combat Regulations*, Nafziger Collection, West Chester, OH (1998)

Strategy and Tactics Staff, *War in the East: The Russo-German Conflict, 1941–45*, Simulations Publications, New York (1977)

Tsouras, Peter G. (ed.), *Fighting in Hell: The German Ordeal on the Eastern Front*, Greenhill Books, London (1995) (Compilation of reprinted US Army studies written by former German officers.)

US Army, *Handbook on USSR Military Forces*, TM 30-430, November 1945.

Zaloga, Steven J. and Leland S. Ness, *Red Army Handbook, 1939–1945*, Sutton Publishing, Gloucestershire, UK (1998)

COLOR PLATE COMMENTARY

A: RECRUIT

This private (1/2) at the war's beginning wears the summer weight 1936 field uniform with 1941 distinctions, i.e., subdued collar tabs. He also wears the Kaska-36 helmet and old-style short marching shoes with puttees. The 1936 field equipment, of which little survived the first year of the war, includes a modern-style backpack, bedroll containing his greatcoat and shelter-cape, ration bag beneath the pack, two-pocket cartridge pouches, entrenching tool, water bottle, and gas mask carrier. He is armed with the 7.62mm Mosin-Nagant M1891/30 rifle with the bayonet reversed in the carrying position. Also shown: a bakelite identification tube (3); a pointed type entrenching tool with carrier (4); an aluminum water bottle and carrier (5); a cartridge bandoleer holding 14 five-round clips (one pictured – 6). Later versions had cloth rather than leather securing tabs. Each of the rifle cartridge pouch pockets held two clips (7); the simple old-style cook pot (8) served as a multi-use cooking and eating utensil; low-topped laced marching boots (9); puttees worn with the low boots (10); BS gas mask and carrier (11) – The horn-like projection between the eyes allowed a finger to be poked in to wipe fogged eyepieces, and scratch the nose. The air-filter is the T-5.

B: LIGHT MACHINE-GUN DRILL

A rifle section had one or two light machine guns crewed by two men. As with most armies, the machine guns provided a base of fire for the section. The crew has scraped hasty positions providing minimal cover. The gunner (1) is armed only with a 7.62mm Degtyarev DP machine gun; he has no pistol. The assistant gunner (2) is armed with an M1891/30 rifle. Later in the war he often carried a submachine gun. The assistant always positioned himself within arm's reach to the gunner's right, a location necessary for belt-fed guns that fed from the right (German and American machine guns fed from the left) and the practice was applied to magazine-fed weapons as well. The assistant carried a metal can holding three 47-round pan magazines. Often the can was used without the canvas case. Commonly only one can was carried. The gunner carried only the magazine fitted to the weapon plus a spare parts and tool kit. The section leader (3) is armed with a 7.62mm Tokarev SVT-40 rifle. While it had been intended as the standard rifle, in some units armed with bolt-action rifles a few of the semi-automatics were distributed through the platoons. The section leader carries a spare ten-round magazine in the leather pouch. Under normal circumstances he used five-round charging clips to load the magazine in the rifle.

Advancing rifle troops halt for a meal break. An M1944 carbine can be seen on the simple backpack in the lower center. On the parapet of an old trench are numerous submachine guns. (Nik Cornish Collection B32)

C: FIELD FEEDING

Taking a break from digging a cut-and-fill trench dugout, these *frontoviki* have been served *borsch* from a PK-43 field kitchen. This wood or charcoal-fired mobile kitchen could cook 66 gallons of soup, stew, or porridge. The four insulated containers were for backpacking 5 gallons of food to frontline positions. The round tin is *tushonka* (stewed pork) while the rectangular tin is Lend-Lease Spam, scooped out with a *finka* knife. Black rye bread was a staple. The soldiers use either the German-style mess kit or the old cook pot. Tin or enameled steel cups were commonly used. Long-handle shovels and pick-axes were available for fortification construction, allowing more efficient work than infantry entrenching tools.

D: FRONT FIGHTER

This corporal (1) in late 1943 wears the 1943 uniform on which rank was displayed on shoulder straps rather than collar tabs owing to the small standing collar. The SSh-40 helmet also saw wide issue by 1942. Submachine guns came into wider use from 1942 and by 1943 large numbers were issued. He is armed with a 7.62mm PPSh-41 with a 71-round drum. A spare drum is carried in a belt pouch along with a three-pocket grenade pouch. By 1944 35-round curved magazines were being issued for the PPSh-41 with a three-pocket pouch and they were also used with the PPS-43 (2). Grenade pouches were widely issued. At the war's beginning a one-pocket pouch was available, here with an F-1 fragmentation grenade (3a). A more practical three-pocket pouch was soon issued, here with an RG-42

fragmentation grenade (3b). The two-pocket pouch was specifically designed for the RGD-33 blast grenade, here with a slip-on fragmentation collar (3c). The ultra-simple backpack (4) was introduced in 1942, and was merely a bag with shoulder straps and a tie-cord. A hatchet with belt carrier (5) was issued to each section; the new type mess kit was based on the German model (6); an issue enameled steel cup (7). Owing to aluminum shortages, glass bottles were issued with cork stoppers (8). As well as green they were issued in brown or clear glass. They could be carried in standard carriers or this insulated type. The BN gas mask had a miter box allowing voice communication and had an improved TSh filter canister (9). The carrier was provided with two side pockets, one for an individual decontamination kit and the other for spare eye lenses and anti-dim cream to prevent lens fogging. A reserve ammunition pouch was carried on the back center of riflemen's belts, holding six five-round clips (10).

E: SCOUTS MANNING AN OBSERVATION POST

One- and two-piece camouflage suits were issued to reconnaissance troops, scouts, snipers, and assault engineers in a variety of patterns. These over-garments were provided

A sharpshooter has obviously been successful in downing a German. The Red Army was comprised of soldiers representing scores of ethnic groups. They wear the baggy camouflage suit with dull black splotches on and olive-drab backing. (Nik Cornish Collection K43)

with integral large hoods to be pulled up over helmets and other headgear. The one-piece suit was known as the *maskirovochnyy kombinezon* (deceptive combination suit) and the two-piece as the *maskirovochnyy kamuflirovannyy kostyum* (deceptive camouflage suit). Both were adopted in 1937/38. Early suits were of flimsy materials lasting only one or two missions. The two-color pattern, known as the "amoeba-pattern" to collectors, consisted of large irregular dark splotches on a lighter background. Early suits were black on olive-brown, but other color combinations were later issued. Late in the war two-color leaf patterns were issued, although they saw comparatively less use. Example camouflage pattern swatches and color combinations are inserted. Another version (not pictured) consisted of a camouflage suit with tufts of strings or fabric strips replicating vegetation sewn about it and called a *mochalniy*. These two *razvedchiki* (scouts) manning an observation post are armed with a 7.62mm PPS-43 submachine gun and a 7.62mm Mosin-Nagant M1938 carbine. One scout observes with 6x B-1 binoculars while the other reports back to the headquarters using a TAM field telephone.

F: DEFENSE OF A BUILDING

Log cabin walls alone were insufficient for cover. Additional support for the walls was installed in the form of bracing logs. Pails filled with sand or water were positioned for fire-fighting and ammunition stocked. Firing positions were dug into the earth floors with earth or sandbags providing additional protection. Earth or logs might be stacked against the exterior wall to protect positions inside. Firing embrasures were cut through logs, or windows were used as firing positions. In some instances trenches ran from the interior positions to the door. Time permitting, trenches also connected buildings. Covered dugouts were built inside buildings for shelter against shelling and would protect occupants from collapses. Positions were also dug well away from buildings, as they served to draw fire. During the spring rains, and even more so during the winter, log cabins were essential for shelter and even survival.

G: INFANTRY WEAPONS

The RM grenade launcher was permanently fixed to the Mosin-Nagant M1891/30 rifle (1). The VGD-30 Degtyarev rifle grenade had a delay fuse allowing it to achieve an airburst. The small grenade was relatively ineffective and was withdrawn in 1943. Specially selected Mosin-Nagant M1891/30 *snaiperskaya* (sniper rifles) were fitted with a turn-down bolt handle and either a 3.5x PU telescope (2a), or the earlier, but less popular 4x PE of 1937 (2b). The Mosin-Nagant M1944 carbine (3) actually began to supplement the M1938 in late 1943 and was fitted with a folding bayonet. The Tokarev SVT-40 semi-automatic rifle (4) was provided with a bayonet with a 9.5in. blade. The PU scope was developed for the SVT. This Shpagin PPSh-41 submachine gun (5) has a 71-round drum, but could use the same 35-round box magazine as the PPS-43. The Sudarev PPS-43 submachine gun (6) was an excellent weapon, but far fewer were produced than the PPSh-41. The Degtyarev DP light machine gun (7) used a 47-round pan magazine. To supplement the DP numerous Degtyarev DT tank machine guns (8) were modified for infantry use by fitting bipods and sights. It used a 60-round drum. The Tokarev TT-33 pistol (9) was issued

Almost 6 million Red Army soldiers ended up in German captivity and over half would die. The Geneva Convention was ignored by both sides.

to officers. A spare eight-round magazine was carried in the holster. The Soviets relied heavily on antitank hand grenades. These heavy impact-detonated grenades could only be thrown 10–15 yards and were stabilized by ribbon streamers when thrown. The RPG-40 (10a) used blast effect to rupture armor. The RPG-43 (10b) was the first to use a shaped-charge warhead. The RPG-6 (10c) was introduced in late 1944 and could penetrate up to 4in. of armor.

H: WINTER

The brutal Russian winter necessitated a variety of special uniforms and components. The Russians, though, were surprisingly ill prepared for their own winter. Some improvements had been made after the 1939–40 Winter War with Finland, but there were still deficiencies. These three soldiers wear the insulated *telogreika* tunic and *vatnie sharovari* trousers, providing a lightweight and relatively warm uniform while allowing freedom of movement. The artificial fur cap, known as the *shapka-ushanka*, had fur-lined flaps for protecting the ears, the sides of the face, and the back of the neck. It came to be a recognition feature of the Soviet soldier. 1 wears issue wool knit gloves and standard boots in which extra foot wraps were worn. The boots may have been lined with newspaper or straw. On his belt are economy canvas cartridge pouches and an RGD-33 grenade without the slip-on fragmentation sleeve. 2 wears the old style *telogreika* with large collars (1 has the newer standing-collar type). The gray greatcoat was essential for protection. The pressed felt *valenki* boots provided excellent foot protection so long as the temperature was well below freezing. They were worthless in wet conditions. He has prized liberated German wool-knit gloves. On his belt with the three-pocket PPS-43 magazine pouch is a popular Finnish *puukko* knife. He is lighting his *makhorka* cigarette with a homemade lighter made from a brass 12.7mm cartridge case. 3 is donning a wool knit protective hood. This was especially useful when wearing a steel helmet, which offered no insulation and even conducted the cold. This *sanitar* (medic) wears the much-valued short sheepskin-lined *shuba* coat. A 5-gallon fuel can, copied from the German design, has been "borrowed" to help start their warming fire.

INDEX